Tarot Forecast 2009

Your Yearly, Monthly and Weekly Prediction
with Remedies

LEO

(July 23 to August 22)

Dr. Seema Midha

HEALTH HARMONY
An Imprint of

B. Jain Publishers (P) Ltd.

An ISO 9001 : 2000 Certified Company
USA – Europe – India

TAROT FORECAST 2009
(LEO)

First Edition: 2008

All rights reserved. No part of this book may be reproduced, stored in a retrieval system or transmitted, in any form or by any means, mechanical, photocopying, recording or otherwise, without any prior written permission of the publisher.

© with the author

Published by Kuldeep Jain for

HEALTH 🌿 HARMONY

An imprint of
B. JAIN PUBLISHERS (P) LTD.
An ISO 9001 : 2000 certified Company
1921/10, Chuna Mandi, Paharganj, New Delhi 110 055 (INDIA)
Tel.: 91-11-2358 0800, 2358 1100, 2358 1300, 2358 3100
Fax: 91-11-2358 0471 *Email:* info@bjain.com
Website: **www.bjainbooks.com**

Printed in India by
J.J. Offset Printers

ISBN: 978-81-319-0653-8

CONTENTS

Publisher's Note 5

Acknowledgement 7

Introduction to Tarot 9

Spreads 12

About the Book 14

Leo Personality 19

Year 2009 for you 21

Monthly Prediction 2009 27

Weekly Prediction 2009 38

Remedies 168

PUBLISHER'S NOTE

With immense pleasure we are introducing this book on 'Tarot Forecast 2009'. Today Tarot science is at its best and people are using its benefits in different ways and modes.

Here we present one of the best solutions offered by Tarot that is prediction of future with the help of Tarot cards. It determines what all can happen in the times coming ahead. This information can be used to mould the things for better results and ways. Not only that, Tarot gives you an insight into obstacles & their best possible solutions. With her knowledge & experience Dr. Seema Midha gives advices and remedies to fight such instances.

Dr. Seema Midha is Asia's one of the famous Tarot card readers and one of the bestselling author of 'Mystical Tarot Deck'. We hope our readers will be benefited by this forecast and enjoy life by referring it.

Kuldeep Jain
CEO, B.Jain Publishers

ACKNOWLEDGEMENT

First and foremost, I would like to thank God Almighty, without whom anything would have not been possible. I am blessed to have such a great family who has been supportive throughout all my endeavors and feats. I would like to thank my publisher who have had the faith in me and given me this wonderful opportunity to come up with this amazing idea. They have been my support system, always showering me with love and giving me the strength to move on and achieve success in whatever I pursue. I would also like to extend my thanks to Aishwarya Ganesh, who helped me a lot. I am truly blessed to be surrounded by such an extraordinary people in my life.

INTRODUCTION TO TAROT

Tarot which is pronounced as 'Taro' refers to the Royal Path. It is a spiritual journey which consists of 78 cards which contains different objects, colours, numbers and symbols. All these cards need to be understood and interpreted so as to get guidance. Tarot reading communicates the meaning because we bring to them our sincere desire to discover deeper truths about our lives.

All cards have different meanings which need to be understood and are related to the situations so as to get meaningful conclusion. Tarot cards prove very helpful when people are in need and dilemma. These cards guide us and prepare us for the coming obstacles in our lives. These are the tools which when believed can change our lives drastically for the positive.

Tarot is a science which helps us sail through the coming obstacles whether day to day or major life problems regarding relations, career, education, job or marriage. Tarot gives positive energy and confidence to face the conflicts that we all face in our everyday lives. Thus, tarot cards help us to emerge as more powerful, strong and a more confident person.

The Tarot deck consists of 78 cards which are classified into major arcana which contains 22 cards and minor arcana containing 56 cards.

The minor arcana is further divided into 4 suits of 14 cards each consisting of 10 pip cards from Ace to Ten and four courts- Page, Knight, Queen and King.

The four suits are Wands, Cups, Swords and Pentacles.

Wands is a fire element card representing ability and determination and the will to succeed.

Swords is an air element card representing forces working against you.

Cups is a water element card representing forces working for you.

Pentacles is an earth element card representing influence of material possessions and monetary benefits.

1. **Pentacles:** Earth element and feminine energy show abundance, prosperity, material, fertility, cultivation, divine path (spirituality) and wealth.
2. **Wands:** Fire held by masculine hands show work that we do, career, progress, fire, zeal, fire burns and progress in work.
3. **Cups:** Water element shows feminine energy that comes from clouds, love, emotions, relationships and partnerships.
4. **Swords:** Air energy indicates mind, thought and intellect. Sword cuts thought in the air. Sometimes, thinking or thought process can also be killing.

Wands – Red and Brown
Cups- Blue and Green
Swords- Cream and Grey
Pentacles- Green and Yellow
Major arcana- Purple and White

We are using our Mystical Tarot Deck for the year 2009 prediction for every Zodiac Sign. The method has been given in sequence.

SPREADS

We use different spreads for different questions. If you want to analyze a specific question in depth, we use specific spreads. We start with the yearly prediction. We explain you how we have provided with our prediction.

Yearly prediction

We start-of by taking out one card representing the overall year prediction for a particular Zodiac Sign. Then, we take out 12 more cards indicating, 12 months for that sign. Later we pick up 5 cards indicating different aspects such as health, money, relations, career and guidance.

Monthly prediction

Then, we pick up 4 different cards indicating each week of the month. Thus, there are 48 cards drawn for 12 months.

Weekly prediction

After the yearly and the monthly predictions, we move on to the weekly prediction. There are 53 weeks in a year. The weekly prediction consists of 13 cards. We take out 1 card indicating the whole week, then 7 different cards indicating each day in that particular week. After the week is over, we draw five more cards each representing:

1. Love
2. Money
3. Health
4. Career, and
5. Education

Also, we have included lucky colours, lucky numbers, lucky days and remedies which can be followed so as to make the week luckier and beneficial.

By this you can come to know how you can take up the opportunity that knocks at your door and also take care of the negative things that can affect you by making the remedial changes.

ABOUT THE BOOK

In this book, we have given you the yearly, monthly and weekly predictions for Leo for the year 2009.

Along with the weekly prediction, we have also provided you with the lucky colours, lucky numbers, lucky days and the remedies in each weekly prediction.

The lucky colours suggest that you shall use the given colour in your daily routine by any means during that week. Different colours help you in enhancing your strength, courage, stability, energy, etc.

For example- The usage of Red colour in our routine gives us vibrant energy, and enthusiasm.

Yellow colour gives us courage and strength.

Pink colour enhances our relations with our loved ones.

The lucky numbers suggest that in a particular week, you shall work with those people whose date of birth matches with the numbers prescribed. Lucky numbers help and guide, for example, when we work with our colleagues, we can deal and mingle with those whose date of birth matches with the lucky number.

People who are planning to buy a house, property or car can buy using these numbers, etc.

The lucky days suggest that you shall complete or initiate new work on the days mentioned. You can plan any trip on these lucky days. If you are buying any car, or any other property on these lucky days, it will prove to be very auspicious.

This helps you to be more prosperous and more confident regarding the task being undertaken.

The remedies which have been mentioned helps you to prepare yourself for the obstacles that may arise and they help you to enhance yourself so that you can enjoy the week even better. A list of remedies has been given at the end of the book.

LEO

(July 23 to August 22)

Your Element: Fire
Your Ruling Planet: The Sun
Symbol: The Lion
Your Stone: Peridot
Life Pursuit: To lead the way
Vibration: Radiant Energy
Leo's Secret Desire: To be a star

Leos have natural leadership qualities as represented by the symbol "The Lion". They enjoy being the centre of attraction and seek praises from others. They have an air of royalty that surrounds them all the time and that is what makes them attractive to many.

They seem to possess a very high parental attitude and take care of their children with intense ferocity. Art and related creative things are best suited for Leos. They love the tasks which allow them to be in the limelight. They are straightforward and love on-stage live performances.

Leo individuals have a great desire to be loved and are mainly characterized by their nature of being vibrant and full of life and spirit. They make sure that they pay importance to the feelings of near and dear ones which definitely sets them apart. They are known to be the good leaders when at work and are also found to be faithful at home. They possess high degrees of charm that they flaunt without any conscious efforts. Leos can cut ties, and leave others heartbroken, but usually there is a good reason why they have broken a tryst. For a Leo, when a relationship is over, really over, it is over for good.

Fire is the element for Leos and this gives them a warm and caring nature. They rely greatly on their instinct as they work without judgment of the situation. They are ruled by the Sun. Thus, they have a desire to be noticed and appreciated. The major point in them is their lively nature and they usually seek support and love from others which help them to move ahead in life.

There can be no better way to reach a Leo's heart other than giving him importance. Leos love elegance and class. They also love receiving compliments. Creative and dynamic in their approach, the Leos are good workers. They work best in high profile jobs where they get the chance of being praised and appreciated well. Doctors, lawyers and executive jobs are perfect for Leos. They also prosper well in the creative field.

LEO

YEAR 2009 FOR YOU

Overview
'Nine of Swords' says that intellect is being utilized effectively throughout the year. There will either completion of knowledge or upgradation of knowledge. There may be less time for relations as the focus is on career. But you will get indecisive or confused regarding your work. Don't get negative thoughts in mind, instead concentrate on the work being done.

Health
'The Judgment card' says that you will experience good health throughout the year as there is faith and belief in God. Spiritual inclination is also indicated. The year is very good as far as health is concerned.

Money
'Queen of Pentacles' indicates that there will be lots of financial and monetary gains. The financial status will also be upgraded. Take advantage of this monetary benefit and make full and correct utilization of it. There

will be shopping and buying of the things but avoid over expenditure and follow a budget.

Relations
'Six of Pentacles' says that you will be very responsible and committed towards your partner and other relations. There is a feeling of give and take in relationships. You will be giving positive energy to your loved ones. You will be successful in maintaining good and cordial relations with everyone.

Career
'Page of Wands' says that this year you will be full of energy and career-oriented. There is enthusiasm, courage and excitement in you to accomplish your work and achieve your targets. You will even get the work of your interest. 2009 is a very positive year for career.

Guidance
In the year 2009, 'Page of Sword' says that you need to use your mind and take decisions wisely. You should not choose the path about which you do not have any knowledge. You should use your energy in the right direction and make full utilization of it.

MONTHLY OVERVIEW 2009

January
'Three of Wands' says that there will be energy, enthusiasm, monetary gains and progress throughout the month. You will work where your interest lies. Thus, you are ready to move ahead towards your goals.

February
'King of Pentacles' says that there will be accomplishment of goals leading to monetary gains. People will also see your dominance, power and authority. But you should not misuse this power; instead put it to correct use. There is an increase in your name and fame, which will lead to recognition at your work place. You may even hold a very big position in your company. You need to be grounded avoiding ego and negative attitude.

March
'Ace of Wands' says that this month, you will be career-oriented which will help you initiate new projects and that will yield you positive outcomes. You need to put in time, energy and mind in your work and also ensure that you take care and nurture the projects you get.

April
'Ace of Pentacles' gives you lots of monetary and financial gains leading to earthly pleasures. There will

be fertility, adversity and prosperity this month with financial gains. You may even get stuck money from any source. It is a good time to buy property.

May
'The Wheel of Fortune' indicates that there will be fluctuations in different aspects of life. You need to carefully analyze each situation by keeping in mind the pros and cons. Your life can get stable by being positive and thus the uncertainties can be changed to certainties. You even need to surrender yourself as there is a spiritual inclination indicated.

June
'Four of Pentacles' says that there is money and prosperity this month. It also indicates that you will be very calculative and evaluating each aspect of the situations. You have to come out of the grid so that positive work takes place. One should not always be disciplined in life rather enjoy the fruits of the hard work done.

July
'Six of Cups' says that there will be exchange and sharing of ideas, thoughts and knowledge. You will maintain good emotional relations with everyone leading to happiness satisfaction and mental peace.

August
'Seven of Swords' suggests that you have knowledge and wisdom but you are not utilizing it in the correct manner. You need to check your planning, organizing of things and implementation of your plans before you move ahead.

September
'Queen of Swords' says that you need to carefully evaluate the positive and negative aspects of life by using your intellect in the right direction. You should approach the problems half-heartedly. Positive outcomes will be experienced only when you work with full energy and mind.

October
'Ten of Pentacles' says that there will be prosperity, monetary gains and material satisfaction. This may lead you becoming self-centred creating disputes due to communication gap. You should not get influenced by others avoiding possessiveness. You may experience disputes related to property.

November
'Four of Swords' says that you are utilizing your intellect and mind in the right direction. You will be waiting for some good news. You are a self-made person who thinks a lot before implementation of plans. Do not act or react, instead wait and watch, you will surely get positive results.

December

'The Fool' says that you will be moving ahead fast with divine powers and spiritualism. There is a new sunrise showing you all colours of happiness. You will be carefree and happy-go-lucky this month. Your focus is on the right direction towards your goals.

MONTHLY PREDICTION 2009

JANUARY

'Three of Wands' says that there will be energy, enthusiasm, monetary gains and progress throughout the month. You will work where your interest lies. Thus, you are ready to move ahead towards your goals.

'Three of Swords' says that in the first week of January there will be collaborations and sharing of work. You will get the opportunity to do good and exciting work. You will be blessed. You may have to change the way you approach the things so as to avoid self-created obstacles. 'Page of Cups' says that in the second week, you will get the offers, you desired in your hand. There will be emotional happiness, contentment, excitement and satisfaction. There will be professional upgradation too. But you need to move slowly so that you can evaluate every step you take. 'Six of Wands' indicates that in the third week there will be achievement of your goals. You will get positive outcomes of the hard work done. You will prove yourself to the world through your work, capabilities and qualities. 'Ten of Wands' says that in the fourth week, your professional image fetches you more work and responsibilities. You will be totally engrossed in your work. But you need to share these responsibilities so that there are fewer burdens on your shoulders.

FEBRUARY

'King of Pentacles' says that there will be accomplishment of goals leading to monetary gains. People will also see your dominance, power and authority. But you should not misuse this power; instead put it to correct use. There is an increase in your name and fame, which will lead to recognition at your work place. You may even hold a very big position in your company. You need to be grounded avoiding ego and negative attitude.

'The Hanged Man' indicates that in the first week, you have to set a level from where you may start making assumptions for yourself. You should accept offers coming your way. You have to be determined while taking decisions unlike a hanged man. 'Nine of Cups' is giving you happiness in the second week. You have confidence in your loved ones that they will support and guide you throughout. 'King of Cups' says you will get emotional offers or offers related to work in the third week. People will come and go in your life this week. But you are not showing your emotions to anyone; rather you should express your feelings and should not be cold to emotions. 'Eight of Pentacles' says that in the fourth week, you will not be ready to share your monetary benefits with anyone. You need to respect others and give unconditional love to those around you so that negativity gets deleted.

MARCH

'Ace of Wands' says that this month you will be career-oriented which will help you initiate new projects which will yield you positive outcomes. You need to put in time, energy and mind in your work and also ensure that you take care and nurture the projects you get.

'The Temperance' card says that there will be a balance of your Karmas. You need to take care of the steps in the same way as a plant would timely needs water and fertilizers to grow. This will ensure security and positive returns. 'Eight of Cups' says that you will not be emotional. You will be detached and leave behind emotions so as to move ahead. 'Two of Wands' says that in the third week, you feel a sense of recognition. People will know you more. This will be due to the love, respect you give to people and also due to the focus towards your work. 'Nine of Wands' says that there will be more work coming your way this week, but due to your experience it will not be difficult for you to accomplish these tasks. It will be a hectic month but due to your planned and organized behaviour you will surpass the obstacles that come in your way.

APRIL

'Ace of Pentacles' gives you lot of monetary and financial gains leading to earthly pleasures. There will be fertility, adversity and prosperity this month with financial gains. You may even get stuck money from any source. It is a good time to buy property.

'Six of Swords' indicates that in the first week, there may be some obstacles in your way but you will face and surpass them with the help of your experience. There will be a need to change your thought-process. 'The Magician' says that you are on the right path and will get positive results. All elements are present around you. There will be completion of your dreams as you have God's blessings. 'Five of Cups' says that you should not get hurt instead take help from others. You should concentrate on your work and should not worry about the results. You have to move ahead with what you have in hand forgetting the past. 'Three of Pentacles' indicates that people will be ready to help, guide and support you and in this process you may get money, if stuck. You need to invest money to create long-term benefits.

MAY

'The Wheel of Fortune' indicates that there will be fluctuations in different aspects of life. You need to carefully analyze each situation by keeping in mind the pros and cons. Your life can get stable by being positive and thus the uncertainties can be changed to certainties. You even need to surrender yourself as there is a spiritual inclination indicated.

'The Emperor' card suggests that in the first week, you will be undergoing thinking process. You will try and help everyone around you. Property, work and relations will be there in your mind. But thinking alone does not work, you need to take initiative and work upon the unhappiness you are facing. 'Five of Swords' indicates that in the second week you will be implementing your plans and will be very action-oriented. There are many things going in your mind as your main focus is short-term gains. You need to think wisely so as to attain long-term benefits. 'Seven of Wands' says that there is a lot of energy and time being used which will yield you positive results. 'King of Swords' says that your status in the fourth week is like a king. There is a balance between thought and mind. You need to enjoy the fruits of the hard work done.

JUNE

'Four of Pentacles' says that there is money and prosperity this month. It also indicates that you will be very calculative and evaluating each aspect of the situations. You have to come out of the grid so that positive work takes place. One should not be always disciplined in life rather enjoy the fruits of the hard work done.

'Two of Swords' says that in the first week, you will not be ready to share your feelings with others though there is mind and thought-process. You may not get the expected results and this may be the reason of your loneliness. The key this week is to share your feelings and problems so as to avoid self-created problems. 'Queen of Wands' indicates that you will experience a very high position in the society in the second week. You will be successful in influencing the environment by not getting affected. There will be a positive force in you which you will be showing to the world. 'The Devil' suggests you not to get deeply attached and engrossed in a particular work. This may even spoil your social image. You should not get influenced by others but should respect other's point of views. 'Three of Cups' says that this is the time to celebrate the fruits of hard work and success achieved. A very enjoyable time is coming ahead. On the whole a very positive time is on your way.

JULY

'Six of Cups' says that there will be exchange and sharing of ideas, thoughts and knowledge. You will maintain good emotional relations with everyone leading to happiness satisfaction and mental peace.

In the first week 'Seven of Cups' says that this is the time to enjoy the rewards. You will see all your dreams coming true this week. This is a very positive time to initiate new projects. 'Eight of Swords' says that you have now closed your eyes and are unable to see the world in front of you. You need to accept the truth and start enjoying life. 'The Chariot' indicates that a new journey towards spiritualism has begun. This also means that there may be a change of place or job. You are ready to move to a new place. 'Eight of Wands' says that you will experience some uneasiness due to the new change. You may have to reorganize everything which will lead to higher responsibilities. But you need to understand that this uneasiness will come to an end as you move forward. For this you also need to set your priorities and move ahead with confidence.

AUGUST

'Seven of Swords' suggests that you have knowledge and wisdom but you are not utilizing it in the correct manner. You need to check your planning, organizing of things and implementation of your plans before you move ahead.

'Knight of Pentacles' says that in the first week, you may experience some stagnation at the start of the work in the first week. This may be because you are not showing what you are doing and vice versa. You need to have confidence in yourself and make wise decisions. 'The Hermit card' says that in the second week, you will try to show light to people with the help of your experiences. In this process you may even get hurt as people may not be too keen in listening to you. You should avoid signing any important documents this week. 'Knight of Wands' says that after a low week, you will see a boost in your energy which helps you get on the right track. You now know what you have to do. A very positive week is being experienced after a negative phase. You will move ahead with full power and zeal towards the accomplishment of your goals. 'The World' indicates that you now know how to understand the world. In this way you will be able to count your blessings.

SEPTEMBER

'Queen of Swords' says that you need to carefully evaluate the positive and negative aspects of life by using your intellect in the right direction. You should approach the problems half-heartedly. Positive outcomes will be experienced only when you work with full energy and mind.

In the first week, 'The Justice card' says that wherever you have put in your time, money and energy, you will see justice and results falling in your favour. 'Two of Cups' says that this week you will be romantic leading to emotional satisfaction. Singles may even come across some one special. The focus now changes from work to relationships. 'Seven of Pentacles' indicates that you need to be action-oriented rather than sitting ideal. You have to use your ideas and thoughts for more progress. You need to reinvest money so that more is generated. 'The Strength card' is indicating that there may be small conflicts and obstacles which you need to solve by making manipulations. This week you will have to butter your seniors so that your work gets completed.

OCTOBER

'Ten of Pentacles' says that there will be prosperity, monetary gains and material satisfaction. This may lead you becoming self-centred creating disputes due to communication gap. You should not get influenced by others avoiding possessiveness. You may experience disputes related to property.

'Page of Pentacles' says that in the first week, you should not overspend money. A budget must be followed so as to avoid overspending. You need to take help and advice from others in order to make better utilization of money otherwise you may even suffer a loss. 'Nine of Pentacles' indicates that there will be lots of monetary benefits arising either by property, investment, share market or lottery. 'Queen of Cups' says that you have to be cautious. You should not trust others easily instead have faith in your abilities and move ahead otherwise you may even lose the monetary gains. Avoid overindulgence of any kind. 'Ten of Cups' indicates that this week, you will enjoy with your family, leading to satisfaction, happiness in relations and at work. You will be able to hit the target this month.

NOVEMBER

'Four of Swords' says that you are utilizing your intellect and mind in the right direction. You will be waiting for some good news. You are a self-made person who thinks a lot before implementation of plans. Don't act or react instead wait and watch, you will surely get positive results.

'The Moon' says that in the first week, you may get egoistic. You know the path towards your destination but due to your ego some third person will take advantage of the situation and move ahead. There may be negative thoughts and doubts arising in your mind which will lead to stagnation of your work. You need to take the initiative and clear all doubts before starting your work. 'The Star card' says that all your hard work has been repaid. This is a time to sit and relax the fruits of your hard work. You will enjoy the colours of happiness. There will be a balance between professional and personal life. It also indicates that you may get involved in a relationship with someone. 'Ace of Wands' says that you will be the ultimate winner. You will see positive results and you will enjoy this success. 'Knight of Swords' says that in the fourth week, you will be highly motivated and moving fast towards your goals. You are in search of knowledge and are rearing to move ahead. You need to move steadily and slowly so that there are long term benefits in this month.

DECEMBER

'The Fool' says that you will be moving ahead fast with divine powers and spiritualism. There is a new sunrise showing you all colours of happiness. You will be carefree and happy-go-lucky this month. Your focus is on the right direction towards your goals.

'Two of Pentacles' indicates that in the first week, there will be obstacles related to work, arising doubts. There will be offers coming and going your way. You need to shortlist the options and choose the correct one. You also need to maintain a budget so that there is enough for future. 'Four of Cups' indicates that you will not be connected with your environment. You will be confused, and indecisive. You may be confused between the opportunities to grab. But you should not lose focus and choose the one which you think will be the most profitable. 'Knight of Wands' says that you will be action-oriented in the third week, giving you positive hope and energy for the future. 'The Sun' indicates that you will earn a bonus due to your hard work. You will prove yourself to the world and attain all happiness leading to more name and fame in this month.

WEEKLY PREDICTION 2009

1st Week
(December 28 to January 3)

Overview

'The Magician' starts the week saying that you will have a remedy with which you will bring smiles to the people. You need to be positive this week and use all the benefits and the gains that you get in the proper way without going into the negative line. You will be taking up the task assigned to you with pride and you will go on in a speeding manner so as to reach your goals on time. You have to slow down during this time so that you get to do your work with perfection. You will be in a cheerful mood and in this way you will enjoy your time with your friends and share some light moments. You will be focused and also emotional during the mid-week. You will be able to take out time for your family and friends too and also satisfy their needs. 'Two of Cups' says that your passion and love towards someone will come out this week. You can even initiate new relations and go for a deeper commitment, if thinking. A short trip or a journey is being indicated this week either related to work or family. You will get to learn and acquire a lot of new things and valuable knowledge during the trip. You need not get egoistic this week as otherwise a third person or a close associate may even take advantage of this attitude and proceed further. You need to be calm and enjoy working. You will be highly romantic during the week-end and you will utilize all the benefits and chances in your favour. Your partner /spouse will be glad and thankful for this romantic behaviour of yours.

Love
'Three of Cups' says that this week, you need to celebrate with your close ones and this moment will be the one to cherish for a long time.

Money
Money matters will be an area to look after. Do not trust anybody blindly as some one may even try to back-stab you and in this, you may suffer to a great extent.

Health
Health will keep you busy this week. You need to go for a check up even if minor problems bother you.

Career
Career will be fine but do not doubt on your self or your colleagues as this attitude may hamper your own growth.

Education
'Queen of Pentacles' is asking you to enjoy the time you spend learning some thing new.

Lucky numbers
1, 3 and 7

Lucky colour
Baby Pink

Lucky days
Wednesday, Thursday and Saturday

Remedies
You have to balance all your energy instead of concentrating only on your love enhancement. You need to set your priorities from time to time and move ahead. Do not choose one single track. Do not sacrifice otherwise it will result in only outflow of money and no inflow of money will take place. You need to keep a Wealth-vase this week at home. (The preparation of wealth-vase is mentioned at the back of this book.)

2nd Week
(January 4 to 10)

Overview
'Four of Swords' says that you have to surrender and understand the depth of every situation before you take the next step. In order to study and get the right idea of your position you have to be attentive and aware. You will be aiming higher this week. You will be satisfied

with the performance till now and now you will be trying to work on some thing new. Do not get negative as people who are jealous of your growth may try and influence you. You need to have confidence in your abilities and trust your own intuitive powers. You may come across some monetary growth this week. 'Knight of Swords' says that you might be moving ahead with having full confidence on your potential. Make sure that you do not ignore the changes that take place in your environment. You may be facing small obstacles but your experience and intellect will definitely come handy and you will be able to clear out all the obstacles with ease. 'The Fool' says that you will be cheerful and ecstatic regarding some new developments and this will keep you interested in your work. You might get highly passionate or negative about a person or task. You shall keep your feelings in limit and always see the positive side of all situations.

Love
You may have to spend some percentage of your income on your loved ones so as to please them and keep them happy.

Money
You will enjoy your monetary position this week. You need to help others and satisfy the needs of your near and dear ones with the help of your monetary gains.

Health

health will be very supportive. You will enjoy and make the best of what you get this week.

Career

You may go in for shortcuts for establishing tasks. But you need to understand that perfection is very important. You need to understand each and every detail before you go in for that work.

Education

'Queen of Swords' says that you might take out time for analysis but this analysis will not be fruitful if you do not get an overview of the situation on the whole.

Lucky numbers

4 and 5

Lucky colour

Chocolate Brown

Lucky days

Sunday, Tuesday and Friday

Remedies

You are likely to become highly possessive this week. You are expecting too much from your close ones and hence you are too sensitive. Do not put too much of intellect into anything. You have to be positive so as to move ahead. You are trying for short earned money this week. You need to take bath from salt water and also clean your house using salt water as it will absorb all the negative energy and make you more positive.

3rd Week
(January 11 to 17)

Overview

'Ace of Wands' says that this week, you are likely to undertake a new line or something new which will be very prosperous for you. You can go ahead and take the job if you are getting a good offer. 'Page of Wands' says that you will be high on energy and vitality. This energy should be used to start a new project this week. If awaiting results, you will get a good score and you will be satisfied with the results. A person close to you will be very helpful this week and you need to take this help with willingness. You can even receive stuck money. You will be elated and happy as you will get a lot time to spend with your family. There will be an emotional flow within you which is likely to come out this week. You will be holding a good position but a delay might trouble you. You need to work hard and stay connected with the surroundings and stay focused. 'Nine of Cups' says that you will be evaluating and enjoying the fruits of the hard work done up till now. 'Eight of Swords' says that you need to interact with people whom you love. You need to exchange ideas and views with them and also take valuable suggestions from them.

Love
You will enjoy the time spent with your family and friends but you can surely enhance your time and moments by taking full advantage of the resources and the environment you are in.

Money
You have to be careful while taking financial decisions as confusions may hamper you. You need to take out time and think deeply.

Health
Your health will be fantastic this week. You will take care of yourself in every possible way and this will give you satisfaction and peace.

Career
A small stagnation is likely to come your way if you do not invest on time. You have to take time and analyze your position from time to time.

Education
'Six of Wands' says that you will be a winner at the education centre this week. You will be recognized for your efforts and in this way students who are waiting for results will get the expected result.

Lucky numbers
3 and 9

Lucky colour
Maroon

Lucky days
Tuesday, Wednesday and Thursday

Remedies
There is a need for upgradation of money matters. You should have full confidence in your abilities and trust your capabilities. You can keep in touch with your mentor so as to take their advice from time to time and get positivism from them. You can even write down the tasks you need to accomplish and read it at least 3 times everyday and work towards it. You will get strength and confidence and in this way your efforts will definitely be appreciated.

4th Week
(January 18 to 24)

Overview
'The Strength' says that you need to be a lot more clever and manipulative if you want to move ahead. You are likely to come across some material and monetary gains and this will keep your spirits high this week. You need

to enjoy these benefits and gains. You will be happy with a continuous inflow of money. 'The World' says that you will be having all the inputs, blessings and the resources so as to prove yourself in a positive way. You will even get a golden opportunity and you will enjoy this time. Your work may take you away from your emotions but you have to understand that this sacrifice will definitely pay you back in the coming future. 'Five of Wands' says that a tough competition is going to come your way this week which will keep you busy. Students will get a good chance to prove their stand. You will be busy tracking and implementing your plans and converting them into paper work. You will succeed in your plans and take the lead. You will have to be aware of what is going around you. You may be getting offers during this week which need to be considered in a positive way.

Love
'The Hermit' says that you shall not go out of the way and help your loved ones as you may not get the expected result.

Money
You are likely to get offers for money enhancements which you shall take up in a positive manner and go ahead.

Health

Health is a matter of concern as you may be thinking about your past and in this way you can get mentally stressed out and tensed.

Career

At the work place, you will hold a great and strong position as it will give you recognition and respect.

Education

'The Hanged Man' says that you are likely to be in a double thought mind and in this way you will be confused. You need to be confident and take time to time advice from elders. Students need to work hard.

Lucky numbers

2 and 9

Lucky colour

Golden Yellow

Lucky days

Sunday, Monday and Tuesday

Remedies

You are content with what you are doing at the work place right now. And in this way you are also not ready to move ahead. You need to enhance your focus and concentration level this week. You can go for a morning walk every day this week and take fresh energy from the nature and be positive.

5th Week
(January 25 to 31)

Overview

'The Temperance' says that you will be in a controlled form and you will be able to strike a balance between your professional and personal commitments. You believe in giving and providing others with their needs and wants. You will be a support to your family. People around you will be happy with your presence and your thoughtfulness. You need to be fast and invest your money in a right manner so that your money grows in the right form giving you high returns. 'King of Cups' says that you need to be expressive and bold. You have to project your true feelings towards people so that people around you get a clear idea of what kind of a person you are. You need to fulfill your wishes and priorities first and then go and help others with their work otherwise you may even neglect yourself and your health will suffer. You will have to work hard towards your ambitions and dreams. You need to put in more efforts for an extra edge over others. You have to be open and flexible so that you get to know about the latest trends and ideas. You will be able to make a difference if you take advantage of the situations and the changes that take place in your environment.

Love
You will be helping others around you so that people around you will get a chance to fulfill their desires. You will support and also teach some useful things.

Money
You need to implement your plans in the right direction so as to gain most of the wealth you have in hand.

Health
'Six of Cups' says that you will enjoy your health this week and people around you will also feel happy with your presence.

Career
You may try to work half-heartedly this week and in this way you may not get the expected results. You need to work by putting in the maximum inputs.

Education
You will be on the top at the education front. Students will be very happy with the results they get this week.

Lucky numbers
5 and 7

Lucky colour
White

Lucky days
Sunday, Wednesday and Friday

Remedies

Career demands a lot of stability. You need to be firm and determined so that you stick to the decisions that you take. You can place a Bamboo plant this week-end in the the north direction or a pair of Blue Dolphin fishes in the north direction for career enhancement.

6th Week
(February 1 to 7)

Overview

'Two of Swords' says that you are being discreet and secretive this week. You need to open up and work harder by getting along with people and exchanging your views with them and in this way, you will also gain a lot and as a matter of fact you will see all the results favouring you. You need to keep away from people who have a negative frame of mind. You will gain if you interact with people from whom you get positive influence. 'The Tower' indicates that you might be sacrificing for others and as a result, you may even ignore your own priorities and aim. You need to keep in touch with your ambitions and aim so as to get them on time. You will be on the right track as you will get the returns for so many sacrifices. You need to learn from the past mistakes and make sure you do not repeat them in future. A total revolution of the situations around you is going to take place in the coming future. You have to be patient and face the obstacles with full patience and confidence. You need to be highly careful regarding investment decisions as you may suffer a loss. You need to be confident and think twice before implementing your ideas. You need to have full knowledge before you take on and work upon a decision as otherwise you are likely to take on the wrong route and you will even end up on the opposite lane. But after so much confusions, you will manage your way out and you will come out on the top with more positive energy.

Love
Lovelife will be amazing this week. You will be enjoying every bit of the time which you spend with your partner/spouse and loved ones.

Money
'Ace of Swords' says that you will be able to manage your finances in a brilliant way. You will enjoy the fruits and the gains.

Health
Health might give you trouble if you take too much pressure on yourself. You need to take rest too.

Career
Career will be very happening this week. You are likely

to get the work of your interest and in this way you will get peace of mind.

Education
You will get passionate about a particular task this week at the education front and you will see that things favour you at the school or other institutes.

Lucky numbers
1 and 2

Lucky colour
Black

Lucky days
Tuesday, Wednesday and Saturday

Remedies
You need to hold the things with maturity this week so that you do not let go the major chances. You need to have stability in life so that you are able to strike a balance. You need to satisfy the needs of your elders and take blessings from them.

7th Week
(February 8 to 14)

Overview
You will be on a high as far as your monetary position is concerned this week. You will be enjoying the luxuries

that you come across and you will even make others a part of your celebration. You will have to be careful while sharing confidential reports with the third person as a close associate can even back-stab you or break your trust. You might be in a confused state but during this time you need to use your experience and intellect in a right way and take out time to analyze the situation and go ahead by being firm. 'Queen of Swords' is asking you to use your analizing power to the fullest so as to gain fully by studying the situation. You need to look at both the positive and the negative sides. You are likely to get offers regarding new job offers or money which needs your time and patience. You can start with a new job or a place as it will give you many more opportunities to prove your capabilities and potential. You will not let down, if you take up these chances and risks. You need to stay positive throughout the week and do not doubt unnecessarily as it will create mental tension. You need to have full trust on your capabilities and confidence. You will be enjoying the fruits of the hard work done till now and you are likely to enjoy the material and earthly pleasure this week-end.

Love

You will see a completion taking place this week. You will be happy and someone of you re-thinking for initiating new relations, then this is the perfect time.

Money
Money matters may be at the top of the list as you will be taking care but you simultaneously need to spend some part of your income on yourself and take out the maximum and also enjoy.

Health
Health will be a matter of concern this week. You need to follow proper medication and do not neglect yourself at any point of time.

Career
You will be successful in implementing your plans at the right time and in this way you will get happiness.

Education
You need to take up the chance which you are getting this week. Education needs time and students need to focus harder.

Lucky numbers
1 and 9

Lucky colour
Peacock Blue

Lucky days
Tuesday, Thursday and Saturday

Remedies
You have to be in a positive frame of mind while taking

up challenges. Do not over burden yourself unnecessarily. You need to recharge your battery and take out time for rest too. You can go for meditation classes or satsang this week which will keep you away from your work for sometime.

8th Week
(February 15 to 21)

Overview

'The Star' says that you will be elated and extremely happy as one of your dearest wishes is likely to come true this week. You will be happy and ecstatic regarding such a high and jovial time. You need to share all your gains and happiness with your close ones and make them a part of your celebration this week. You need to be among people and have faith in your close ones. You will be benefited, if you take up the opportunity to interact and mingle with people. You will get to know about the positive and the negative aspects of your point of views. You will hold a good and a strong position if you utilize all the resources in your favour. People will follow your commands too. A third person who is close to you will definitely come to your help and one of your stuck work will go on smoothly with this help. You need to be in touch with your surroundings this week.

LEO

You need not help others by ignoring your own tasks. You may not get the response which you are looking forward to. You should rather take on your tasks and work upon your ideas. At the end of the week you will see that there will be a flow of happiness in this week and you will be glad as you are going to have a splendid weekend.

Love
'Six of Wands' says that you will be ecstatic regarding your Lovelife. There will be something new taking place this week.

Money
You shall not be in haste while taking investment decisions. You need to take proper care before you end up on the conclusion.

Health
Health is likely to give you tension this week too. You have to take proper care as if you do not give full attention then minor problems will take a bigger step.

Career
You need to surrender yourself as you need to take out time to study each and every aspect of the task assigned to you.

Education
You will enjoy studying this week. You will take keen interest in the subjects that you study this week.

Lucky numbers
6 and 8

Lucky colour
Grey

Lucky days
Tuesday, Thursday and Saturday

Remedies
Your money is likely to get blocked if you do not take prior care. You may have to wait for the results. You also need to move ahead at a slow and steady pace. You can plant trees and as the plant grows you will see a positive environment around you. You will sense a positive feeling of healing and satisfaction.

9th Week
(February 22 to 28)

Overview
You will be giving a lot this week. People around you will be thankful as their wishes are granted because of you. Do not take decisions in haste as it will lead to a problem and unwanted tension. You need to keep in control and take full information before you take up any decision. 'Three of Swords' says that you need to stay positive this week so as to maximize profit. You

might create trouble for yourself if you do not take things with a positive attitude. You will be able to balance your energy this week within and outside your office premises. You are likely to go on a trip this week and this trip can give you many chances to learn new things. You need to stay confident. You need not get egoistic this week as in that case a third person will take the advantage and lead. You need to concentrate on your tasks and move ahead with a positive and a firm frame of mind. You may have to be clever so that your work does not stop in the middle. You will have to apply or try the other route so that you are able to go on without any stagnation. 'The Tower' says that you might have to sacrifice this week. But this compromise will give you a better chance to come up on the top.

Love
'Nine of Cups' says that you will be enjoying each and every moment to the depth. You will see a positive support from your partner/spouse.

Money
Money matters needs time this week. You might see a turnover in the current position. Stay calm and invest after deep inspection.

Health
Health is likely to suffer this week. You shall not keep your past in your mind as in that case you will be unable

to move ahead with a positive aura. Stay positive as it will reflect in your health.

Career
You will be working hard and vigorously but these efforts will definitely not go in vain.

Education
'Three of Cups' says that at the education centre you will see enjoyment and celebration. Those who are planning to take a break, this is the perfect time.

Lucky numbers
3 and 7

Lucky colour
Lemon Yellow

Lucky days
Tuesday, Wednesday and Friday

Remedies
A big problem may trouble you this week. You need to stay calm and cool. This change will definitely affect you but your attitude will also have a big role to play. You have to be courageous and bold. You need to have clarity in your thoughts too. For peace and balance of thoughts, you practice Yoga this week. You need to take the initiative and move ahead with a positive attitude.

10th Week
(March 1 to 7)

Overview
'Page of Cups' says that you will be energetic and enthusiastic. You will take full interest and pride in the tasks that you take up this week. You will be happy with the results that you face this week and as a result you will take out time to make new aim. You need to plan this week. You will be happily enjoying the rewards that come your way and as a result you can plan out some shopping or outing plan. Spend within limits this week. Some delays might trouble you this week. You need to have patience and strike at the right time without losing aim. You will be high on energy and passion. New tasks can be taken and given a chance. Students can take part in other activities and take pleasure out of it. You might have to move away from your emotions if you want to accomplish your tasks this week. You shall not lose hope as you will get a lot of time to spend with your family. 'Ten of Wands' says that you might be taking lots of responsibilities at a time which might result in tension and fatigue. You need to prioritize your tasks and share your responsibilities with your colleagues too. Have full and deep knowledge before you take up any further step. You are full of energy, so do not misuse this energy in the wrong direction.

Love
You will be going towards a deeper commitment this week. Singles are going to find their soul-mates.

Money
You will be satisfied with the way your financial position is proceeding. You will be careful regarding the steps that you take.

Health
You will take care of others and this in return will give you positive vibes and you will be enjoying your health too.

Career
'The High Priestess' says that you need to put that extra efforts and make your plans to take place. Apply your plans and thoughts to paper so that you do not get disappointed.

Education
You will have to be expressive. You need to project your feelings and your thoughts. Be innovative and creative this week.

Lucky numbers
2 and 5

Lucky colour
Sea Green

Lucky days
Sunday, Monday and Wednesday

Remedies

You need to split your time and balance your energy this week in every direction. Set your priorities and work accordingly. You need to hold the hard earned money in the right direction. You are an excellent giver but you also need to understand that sometimes in relations you also need to accept things from others.

11th Week
(March 8 to 14)

Overview

You have to open up this week. You need to utilize the opportunity that you get to advertise your thought in front of your loved ones. You are full of elements and the resources that you need this week. You have to use these elements to your favour and make the most of it. You will be successfully planting your plans in the right direction. You will be content with the way you work from now onwards. You will be the centre of discussion wherever you go this week. People around you will be highly pleased with your presence. Your presence of mind will also be appreciated. 'The Fool' says that you will be cheerful and happy this week. You will also be carefree and enjoy the light moments with your friends. Your analysis will not prove you wrong this week. You will be highly evaluative and calculative this week. You need to be mature while taking investment decisions, otherwise you are likely to take the wrong path. You need to be active and take decisions on time without thinking much.

Love
'The Emperor' says that you will be taking the charge but do not impose your thoughts on others as that will not give you any pleasure.

Money
'Ace of Cups' says that you will be enjoying the monetary and the material wealth this week and you will be keen to spend some money on your loved ones too.

Health
Health will be extremely supportive and you will not be let down from your health point of view.

Career
You have to come out of a frame which is binding you. If you come out then only you will be able to check your position and move forward with time.

Education
You will be at the top as people around you will see you as an influential character. You will not hesitate in helping others this week.

Lucky numbers
1 and 4

Lucky colour
Saffron

Lucky days
Sunday, Monday and Tuesday

Remedies
Though you are giving, you are not happy. You need to go for an outing this week with your family and friends and enjoy light moments. You have to take out time for your loved ones this week and be more flexible instead of rigid.

12th Week
(March 15 to 21)

Overview
Students who are awaiting results will be able to hear good and positive results. You shall not go in for shortcuts as then you will get only short-term happiness. You need to work for long term goals this week. You shall put on more inputs from your side so as to get the exact and accurate results. You will be helping others with what you have in hand this week. Your loved-ones will be thankful and appreciating your efforts. You need to be fast in terms of taking financial decisions as

if not, there will be stagnation and hence you may find it difficult to move ahead with smoothness. 'Ace of Swords' says that in particular you will come out on top and enjoy the position that you get this week. You will be respected and regarded for the efforts that you put in. Those who are fighting legal matters will get a ray of hope this week and this will give them positive vibe for the future. You need to avoid being in the company of those who discourage you. You need to have faith in your abilities and move ahead with a positive energy.

Love

'The Lovers' says that though you will be highly passionate and considerate you might have to stay away from your loved ones for some time.

Money

You will be in a charge this week. Money matters will be at the top of the priority list this week.

Health

'The Devil' says that you need to take full care of your health this week as you are likely to suffer a lot. You need to make sure that you follow the medication process.

Career

You need to get away from the past if you want to move ahead with your plans. You need to be positive and detach yourself from your past.

Education

'The Hanged Man' says that a confused state may hinder you this week. You need to have trust in yourself and go on with your potentials and plans.

Lucky numbers
5 and 6

Lucky colour
Peacock Blue

Lucky days
Tuesday, Thursday and Friday

Remedies

Health needs care this week. You can donate and help the poor people who cannot afford to buy medicines this week and help them become more stable and healthy. You will enjoy your health if you help some one lead a better life.

13th Week
(March 22 to 28)

Overview

'Ten of Wands' starts of this week saying that you are trying to take most of the responsibilities on yourself leading to stress and tension. You need to set your priorities and go ahead by distributing these tasks with others too. You will be emotional at the start of the week which will keep you on a high. You will seek mental support from your loved ones. You need to implement your plans and your ideas and take action at the right time. You shall take one thing at a time if you want perfect results without delay. 'Two of Wands' says that you will be busy as you will take out time to plan your further steps. Businessmen need to make further plans so as to expand their work. This is the perfect time as you will flourish if you take up a new challenge during this time. You need to take up the offer which is knocking at your door as it will help you project your talent and true colours in front of the world. You will be benefited if you eat up the offers with a positive attitude by forgetting your past. You will enjoy the weekend among many people as your loved ones will have an amazing time which they will spend with you. You will be the main topic in discussion as people might even discuss your achievements.

Love
You will be satisfied with your partner/spouse response to you on various issues and matters. You will enjoy the time you spend with your loved ones.

Money
'Page of Wands' says that you will be energetic and deeply involved in those matters concerning finances.

Health

You need to take care of your health though you will be active.

Career

'Nine of Cups' says that you will be analyzing your performance till now and you will be enjoying your fruits of the hard work.

Education

You need to keep intact with your aim so that you do not get deviated from your path. You need to have full information about the path that you take up this week so as to go on the right direction.

Lucky numbers

1 and 2

Lucky colour

Red

Lucky days

Monday, Thursday and Saturday

Remedies

Though there is enthusiasm there is an urgent need or upgradation this week. You can attend classes and learn through them. You need to take suggestions from elders and move under their guidance. If any confusion strikes your mind, you can consult your seniors.

14th Week
(March 29 to April 4)

Overview

You need to be highly careful this week as people around you can try to take undue advantage of you and your sincerity. You need to maintain some distance with everyone especially at the work place. The week starts on a high and a bright note as you will see an almost dream coming alive. You will be extremely happy with the way things turn out for you this week. You will be sharing your experiences with your colleagues and loved ones. You will see positive results for the work and efforts put up till now and you will be highly convinced by the outcomes. You need to escape from people who do not match up to your positive level. You need to be in the company of people who are positive and have an encouraging frame of mind. 'Eight of Swords' says that you need to have trust and confidence in yourself so as to move ahead with a positive force. You will definitely see a ray of hope if you get along with people and enjoy the company of people. You will be enjoying the respect and the position you get this week at the work place and at home. 'Three of Wands' says that after much evaluation of all the past work, you will be happily coming towards your next goal this week. 'The World' says that you will be having the blessings of the entire masculine and the feminine powers which need to be used in a positive way. You can initiate new work or new relations this week.

Love
You might get either too negative or too passionate about someone close. You need to express your feelings in limit so as to get the right kind of response.

Money
A past investment is likely to come and give you high returns this week. There is a complete cycle being indicated.

Health
Your health might suffer if proper care is not taken. You need to follow proper medication if you want to see yourself fit and healthy.

Career
'Two of Swords' says that you need to be interactive and communicative this week so as to see results in your favour. You have to open up with your colleagues.

Education
'The Hanged Man' says that double-thoughts may haunt you this week regarding upgradation but you need to stay calm and give ample time to each situation and you will get the answer on your own.

Lucky numbers
2 and 8

Lucky colour
Black

Lucky days
Sunday, Monday and Saturday

Remedies
Do not get possessive regarding your love matters or money. You might even become dominant and in this way your close ones may not get their space and respect. You have to change your attitude completely this week to the positive. Do not get bonded up with chains of relations. You are spiritual, thus you need to take out time for spiritualism and for yourself. There has to be exchange of energy this week with others.

15th Week
(April 5 to 11)

Overview
'Knight of Cups' says that you will be focused and emotional at the same time. You will be able to maintain a balance between your personal and professional commitments. You will be seen as a teacher this week. People around you will come up to you and seek lessons

from you. You will have to be highly careful while signing important contracts and deals so that all terms and conditions are clear and fine. You will see a big turnover of the conditions in front of and you will see a transformation this week. Something unexpected will happen which will need your time. 'Knight of Pentacles' says that you will have to look at your performance so that you do not fall short of the inputs. You need to invest during this time so as to take full advantage of the situations in your favour. You will have to surrender yourself so that you get to realize where you are going wrong this week. You need to be aware of your shortcomings this week. Though you will be highly emotional you need to show and express your feelings in front of others so that others get to know about how you feel. By the end of the week, you will see a big monetary gain coming in your hand this week. You will be highly excited and elated by this income.

Love
You may be in an indecisive mood this week. You need to discuss the problems with your family and close ones and take out time so as to welcome suggestions from others.

Money
You will be moving ahead and enjoying the pleasure of the monetary and the material gains.

Health

'Five of Cups' says that you need to get detached from your past so as to move ahead with a positive frame of mind otherwise you will definitely get bogged down with worries and tension.

Career

Career will see some action this week. There will be some competition or examination which you will have to go through so as to come on the top.

Education

'Three of Cups' says that education side will flourish this week. You will be at the top and you will see a big occasion to celebrate.

Lucky numbers

4 and 5

Lucky colour

Golden Yellow

Lucky days

Sunday, Monday and Saturday

Remedies

You may get indecisive and confused this week, so as to avoid conflicts in mind. You shall not think negative about any opportunity as you will get a chance to prove your abilities and you need to take up the challenge. Do not deviate from your path and be focused. You have to surrender your self to the tasks that you take up. You need to chant Mantras this week as you will get positive vibe through this and as a result you will be able to see your way through.

16th Week
(April 12 to 18)

Overview

'The Lovers' says that this whole week you will be romantic and passionate about your lover. You are likely to head for a deeper commitment this week and you will not be disappointed. You need to analyze the situations on the whole, so that you get an overview of the case and then only you will be able to get the real idea. You may be sad as people around you may not respond the way you wanted for the help you give them. You shall not get depressed and concentrate on your tasks and do not waste your time on others. You may get delayed while reaching your goals. You need to show more willingness and determination as you will be able to reach your targets on time. 'Six of Swords' says that small initial problems are likely to come on your way but you need to be determined and calm. Your experiences will come and prove you very useful during this time. You need to change your outlook towards other things and people so as to derive better conclusions. You have to get adaptable to the changes that you face. 'The Sun' says that you will be extremely happy with the changes and the way you and others perceive these changes. You will see support from others and you will be on a high during this time. 'The Fool' says that you will be highly elated and energetic at the end of the week. You will see many new changes favouring you.

Love
You will have all that you want during the week but you need to realize this fact and work accordingly towards your love life.

Money
'Queen of Cups' says that you might get negative about the gains that you get this week. You need to stay positive and do not get influenced by others.

Health
Health will be perfect this week and you will go on smoothly with your work, your personal commitments and your health are not giving you much trouble.

Career
'Ten of Pentacles' says that you have evaluated much and now is the time to implement your plans and ideas so as to see the returns.

Education
'Ace of Swords' says that you will be an over all winner at the education side and you will enjoy the time studying and taking part in other activities.

Lucky numbers
4 and 6

Lucky colour
Saffron

Lucky days
Monday, Friday and Saturday

Remedies
Do not trust others easily as investment plans can take the wrong route. You need to be in touch with your nature and take advice from others on time. You need to listen to others but ultimately follow your own heart. You may not be getting back the stuck money so you have to think twice before applying your knowledge. You can keep the Vishnu Kalash this week at home and as a result you will get stability at home. (The preparation of Vishnu Kalash is mentioned at the back of the book)

17th Week
(April 19 to 25)

Overview
'Seven of Swords' says that you might end up on the wrong side this week if you do not look after the steps that you take this week. You need to take full care of the further decisions that you take. You need to maintain a positive outlook so that you do not doubt unnecessarily and move ahead with energy and a vibe. You need to stop sacrificing for others as you will not be gaining out of it. You need to work for your own needs and wants. 'Queen of Pentacles' says that you will take out some time to spend some money on yourself and you will also pamper yourself. You need to spend within limits. You will also take out time for your family. You will be having a great time and satisfaction in your way. You might be getting offers and money benefits which you need to take up for further enhancements and advancements. You need to take out time and spend some money on yourself this weekend. You have the right to enjoy the fruits and the benefits that you get. You will also be showered with more monetary benefits and you need to take proper investment decisions.

Love
'The Judgment' says that people surrounding you will

be happy with your presence, they may even involve you in important decision making time.

Money
You are likely to receive stuck money this week and a third person may even help you get this money. Money matters will be good.

Health
'Ace of Cups' says that this will be a highly emotional week and this will reflect in your behaviour in a positive way.

Career
You might have to pay more attention towards tiring career this week. You need to be more willing while taking up responsibilities at the work place, as a result you will get a chance to prove your abilities.

Education
'The Empress' says that you will be a helper and a giver this week. You are likely to share the resources, elements and the inputs that you have in hand with others and gain mental peace. During this process, you will be able to gain knowledge from others too.

Lucky numbers
3 and 7

Lucky colour
Pink lotus

Lucky days
Tuesday, Wednesday and Saturday

Remedies
You are being emotional while taking career options this week. There is a lot of emotional turmoil this week and in this way you may be unable to concentrate on your work. You need to understand that everything is temporary in this world and sometimes you also need to focus on your future karmas and work in a positive way. You need to forget if you want to move ahead. You can wear Pink Quartz bracelet so as to enhance your relations.

18th Week
(April 26 to May 2)

Overview
'Page of Pentacles' says that you will be cheerful and ecstatic regarding the up coming projects but you need to deal with these projects with maturity as immaturity may lead to some wrong decisions. You will be analytical and calculative this week. You will be happy as your analysis will take you one further step towards

your aim. You need to work with full concentration and dedication without thinking much about the results. You will be emotionally bound with someone. You might even go for a deeper commitment and singles may find someone interesting. You will be seeing victory in a particular field this week. You will be satisfied with the results. 'Six of Cups' says that you will be helping others and serving them with what you have in hand. People around you will be satisfied with your presence. 'The Moon' says that you shall not get egoistic as if you do become egoistic a third person who has been giving you competition will take the lead and you might even suffer the loss. You need to stay positive and have confidence in your abilities and do not think about the progress of others. 'The Strength' says that this week, things may not move the way you wanted and as a result, you may have to take the other course or other trick so that your work moves on in the right direction.

Love
'Knight of Swords' says that you might be moving ahead at a very fast pace. You need to give an equal chance to others to respond on time.

Money
You will be in a good strong position at the monetary side, but you need to share these benefits and gains with others so that you do not get possessive.

Health
'The Chariot' says that you will be moving in the right direction at the right pace while enjoying the luxuries that come your way. You will enjoy a good health.

Career
You will be guiding others this week at the work place. You will get mental satisfaction as your experience is now coming handy.

Education
You need to be more action-oriented this week at the studies side so as to gain. You have to take proper steps at the right time.

Lucky numbers
6 and 7

Lucky colour
Forest Green

Lucky days
Tuesday, Wednesday and Thursday

Remedies
You may be moving a bit fast this week. Do not ignore other valuable things during this week otherwise you are likely to lose some good opportunities. You need to move at a slow and a steady pace so that you get ample time to analyze the situations. You can place a golden wind-chime at your house for a positive flow of vibe

and energy. You can even go to the school and distribute chocolates among children as you will get good wishes.

19th Week
(May 3 to 9)

Overview

'Seven of Swords' indicates that you need to be highly careful this week while taking on tasks on yourself as in by over-burdening yourself, you are likely to move in some other direction. You need to keep your aim in your mind and move accordingly. You have to take steps so as to spend some part of your income on your personal enhancement. You have the right and you deserve this enhancement and advancement step. You will be holding a strong position this week at the work place which will give you command and respect. Your subordinates will take suggestions from you and this will also keep you high. You will be evaluating your performance till now and after much inspection you will carry on aiming further. You shall be more sharing especially regarding the monetary and the material gains that come in your hand. 'Five of Swords' says that you have to be more specific as far as your tasks are concerned. You need to set your priorities and move slowly by analyzing the changes in the situations at the right time. You will take out time to study the plans that you have kept in mind. You will gain if you keep going further with these plans.

Love
There are some decisions either pending or confusing this week. You need to be calm and discuss these matters with your loved ones so as to have a clear vision.

Money
Money matters will be good but can be improved if you utilize what you have in hand in a proper way.

Health
Health needs attention this week. Do not be adamant as it will not do you any good.

Career
Career front will be fantastic this week. You will be using your intellect and talents in a right manner and you will be able to judge your position in a right manner.

Education
You will move ahead with a positive force. For students, this is a positive time to undertake any new enhancement course.

Lucky numbers
3 and 7

Lucky colour
Chocolate Brown

Lucky days
Monday, Tuesday and Saturday

Remedies
You have to work on decision-making this week. There has to be attitude and gratitude from your side as you have everything. There is a right time needed when you need to strike. You need to care and nurture all that you have in hand. You can keep a Pyramid this week at the work place and at home so that you are grounded every time. You will see a smooth and a stable life.

20th Week
(May 10 to 16)

Overview
You need to be more analytical this week so as to gain in the right form. You are not utilizing all your energy in a right manner. You are tending to go out of the way in order to help others. But this will give you less satisfaction or no satisfaction. You need to be more specific and lend help to only those who value your words. You are likely to experience a delay in your work this week which might keep you tensed. You shall not get upset as good time is on its way and you will surely

get a bright chance. You are going to face some initial hurdles in your way which you will be able to clear out with the help of your close ones. 'Four of Pentacles' says that you have to come out of a fixed frame of mind to accept and welcome changes so as to apply the changes in your daily life and move with time. You need to get detached from your past in order to move ahead with a positive attitude. You will gain if your past is forgotten as in the present you may not realize that you have everything in hand. Do not over-pressurize yourself as it will give you unnecessary tension. You need to share these tasks with your colleagues and your juniors. 'Eight of Cups' says that you might have to move away from your emotions due to work as a trip is indicated.

Love
You are likely to get a proposal this week from a secret admirer which you need to consider.

Money
'Eight of Wands' says that you shall not be in haste to undertake any investment project under the influence of others. People are likely to influence you in a negative way.

Health
'The Star' says that you will be as bright as the star this

week. You will enjoy every moment to the fullest and enjoy your health.

Career
Career front may see you being secretive. In an organization, you need to be with and among people so as to proceed further. You need to project your ideas so that others get a favour of your thinking too.

Education
You need to go ahead and take up the course which is in your mind. This is a highly prosperous time for all students.

Lucky numbers
6 and 8

Lucky colour
Aqua Marine

Lucky days
Sunday, Monday and Friday

Remedies
You may be unable to see all the things despite the fact that you have everything in hand. As you are trying everything at a time, everything may seem blocked. You need to have trust in your abilities in such a way that you take on specific tasks and work upon them wholly. You need to write down your wish on a White sheet of paper with a red pen and read it thrice a day so as to

gain energy from it. For career, enhancement you can wear a Blue bracelet as it will give you vision and clarity of thoughts.

21st Week
(May 17 to 23)

Overview

'The Hierophant' says that this week, you will use most of your energy while helping and guiding others in such a manner that others gain a lot from your teachings. You need to surrender yourself to your own tasks too at some point of time. Those who are waiting for results might have to wait for some more time. You are full of bright ideas and plans in mind which need to be implemented at the right time for prosperity. You will gain if you do not lose this opportunity. Your giving and helping nature will continue for sometime and people around you will be impressed by your efforts. 'Queen of Pentacles' says that you might be in a spending mood this week. You are likely to take out some percent of your income and use it for personal use. You will be enjoying your time with your family and friends and this will give you mental satisfaction and peace. You have to leave the results on God as you have done your side of hard work. 'Ace of Cups' says that at the end of the week, you are likely to notice a high emotional flow inside you and you will be romantic this week. You can even confess your love to someone close and initiate new relations.

Love
You need to take care. Make sure you think before you say as someone is likely to get hurt by your words.

Money
'The Tower' says that money matters can see a downfall if you go on helping and serving others and their needs with your money without fulfilling your own needs and wants.

Health
'The Chariot' says that your spiritualism inclination will keep you in high spirits and you will see mental peace. You will enjoy good health.

Career
You will be enjoying the time working at the work place and you will even get appreciation for the work done.

Education
You will take full and deep interest in studying the subjects of your interest. New activities should be tried during this week as you are full of vitality and passion.

Lucky numbers
2 and 6

Lucky colour
Magenta Pink

Lucky days
Tuesday, Thursday and Saturday

Remedies
There is an excess of everything this week. You may not be on the right path as you have lost control. You may even suffer a downfall if you do not stop sacrificing. You have to read and sign the deals during this week. You need to do the work in writing this week. You have to be patient so as to get positive results. You can use metallic coins by keeping them with you and also keep a lucky charm with you as it will give you strength and energy.

22nd Week
(May 24 to 30)

Overview
This week is prosperous as far as your money prospects are concerned. You can make future investment, or property as in the future you will get high returns due to such decisions. You will be evaluating your performance till now and you will not be disappointed. You will also enjoy the benefits and the fruits of the

efforts that you have put in till now. You need to express your desires and the feelings that you have in mind and heart. You need to be interactive this week. You will get passionate regarding some one close and this will evoke romance in you. 'Ten of Swords' says that you need to be careful as people around you might even take undue advantage of you and break your trust. You shall not get into office gossip this week as it will backfire at you in some time. You will see some financial gains coming your way this week which will keep your spirits high and energetic. You will be enthusiastic. You need to make sure that you put these benefits to the right use. Do not readily help others at the cost of your health or your priorities. You will be able to strike a balance between your professional and personal obligations. You will be spiritual this week.

Love
You will be full of vitality and energy. You will be moving ahead with a positive frame of mind.

Money
You need to spend money on yourself this week. You need to share and exchange ideas with others regarding finances.

Health
Health will be odd and on the top. You will enjoy the

week to the fullest. You will even go on and take care of those who are sick or ill.

Career
A big change is likely to come your side at the career front. You need to see and notice the changes and work accordingly without losing hope.

Education
Education needs your 100 % attention this week. You have to put in more efforts so as to move ahead.

Lucky numbers
6 and 9

Lucky colour
Peacock Blue

Lucky days
Tuesday, Thursday and Saturday

Remedies
You need to take the initiative this week so that you get to work. You may notice that the doors have been closed. You have to market your capabilities so that you get the desired results. Do not be indecisive as you will be wasting your time and energy. You can wear a metal Kada in your left hand as it will make you more committed towards your job. You will be able to make the right usage of your money and energy.

23rd Week
(May 31 to June 6)

Overview

'The Fool' says that you will be full of positive energy and vitality and you will want to move ahead with a positive vibe. At the start of the week, be careful as your trust can be broken. You need to take care before signing important papers. You will be romantic this week. As you will seek emotional satisfaction and you will see that your partner will surely support you. 'Knight of Cups' says that you will be focused and energetic this week. You may not allow your emotions to take over your work. You will continue to work in the same manner. You may have to go the other way so as to complete the work as the right method may not come handy. A person who was not very helpful or trustworthy will be of extreme importance now. You will be on the right path, after getting a start you will go on to and take on the further step. Make sure you notice the changes that take place in your environment during this course of time. You will be facing a competition or an examination this week which will keep you busy and occupied. You need to face the exam with courage and determination. You will see a completion taking place this week. This is the perfect time to start on with a new project and flourish.

Love

Lovelife may be in troubles this week. You need to give space and time to all your relations so that you get to evaluate them on time. Do not get highly negative or over possessive.

Money

You will see a result to the investment this week. You will enjoy the results.

Health

'Seven of Pentacles' says that though you are not likely to face any big trouble from the health side, you can surely avoid dullness by being active.

Career

You will see a helping hand this week at the career front and you will be able to complete your work on time with this help.

Education

Education needs time and patience. You need to take time so that you do not get confused at any point of time.

Lucky numbers

2 and 5

Lucky colour

Purple

Lucky days
Monday, Tuesday and Saturday

Remedies
You need to be confident and keep your options ready and open. You need to be interactive this week. You are enjoying the earthly pleasures and projecting yourself in the wrong manner. You have to take up the responsibility and move ahead with fulfilling your commitments. You should cherish small moments. You can be thoughtful and gift your close ones with what they want.

24th Week
(June 7 to 13)

Overview
'Ace of Wands' says that this is a highly positive and a prosperous week for you. You will be on the top as far as your education and self-enhancement is concerned. You will be one of the most important persons wherever you go this week. You will be appreciated for your efforts and ambitions. You shall not doubt anybody unnecessarily as this doubt may not allow you to move ahead with a positive frame of mind. You shall be mind oriented and do not come under the influence of other people. 'Ten of Pentacles' says that you need to be more

active in terms of finances. You need to take fast decisions without making any delays. You will be bright as the Sun and people will surely look up to you as an influential person. You will be adored for your efforts and outlook. You will get a lot of time to party and celebrate a recent victory. You are likely to come across good news. You need to make investment plans as now your work needs your money too. If you do not make the necessary arrangements then you are likely to get stagnated. At the end of the week, you will be happy and merrily enjoying with full of energy and enthusiasm.

Love
You will be at the top in your relation this week. You will get the maximum satisfaction and all the things will fall in place.

Money
'King of Swords' says that you will not leave any scope for any mistake and you will take full care while taking financial decisions.

Health
Your Health will suffer if you do not keep your ego aside and you need to take care of yourself without letting the negativity affect you.

Career

'Seven of Wands' says that this week will be hectic and full of action. You will be seeing positive results for the hard work done.

Education

'Two of Wands' says that you will be enjoying your time at the education centre and taking positive steps towards your aim.

Lucky numbers

1 and 6

Lucky colour

Bright White

Lucky days

Sunday, Wednesday and Thursday

Remedies

Health needs time this week. You have to take care of your health by regular check-ups. You can be in a positive environment this week. You have to build up a strong and a positive surrounding. You can donate White clothes or Milk products or Coconuts in the temple this week. You will definitely see a positive change in your health.

25th Week
(June 14 to 20)

Overview

'Nine of Wands' says that you will be taking out time so as to implement your plans on time which would mean that this week, you can even start of with past pending decisions as you have the courage and the power. You need to put in your efforts and plans with full concentration, focus, determination and dedication, without thinking much about the results. You will have to be a lot more active in terms of taking quick investment decisions this week. You may be wasting your time by evaluating your gains and benefits. You need to use your energy in a better way. You will be moving ahead with the right spirit and at a fast pace. You should notice the changes that continuously take place in your environment. You will be energetic and enthusiastic regarding finances and the upcoming work. You will be analyzing the way you have been working till now. You will share your gains and benefits with others as it gives you pleasure and peace of mind. 'The Sun' says that you will enjoy a good position which will give you respect and you will also be influential for others. You will also enjoy the weekend.

Love
This is the perfect time to enhance and start with new relations as they will bloom and prosper in the coming future.

Money
You will be enjoying the monetary position this week. You are likely to acquire a status or a position by utilizing your money.

Health
You will be fine at the health. Your health will support you throughout the week.

Career
'Four of Pentacles' says that your ideas may be fixed this week at the career front which might not allow you to work with flexibility.

Education
'Knight of Pentacles' says that you may feel stagnated as you are not putting the desired amount of inputs or efforts.

Lucky numbers
1 and 6

Lucky colour
Red

Lucky days
Monday, Tuesday and Saturday

Remedies
You may fix some of your ideas at the career front. You need upgradation this week and you need to learn new things. You have to be positive in your thought-process and listen to others too.

26th Week
(June 21 to 27)

Overview
'Page of Wands' indicates that this week, at the education point of view, students will be fair well and will be able to perform as per the expectations. You need to have realistic aims and your power and focus will definitely see you through. You need to be highly careful while discussing important topics with your close associates as people around you might try to take undue advantage of you. You will be able to solve all the hurdles that come your way and in this way you will see yourself at the top. You need to be strong and determined. A third person this week will be very helpful to you. Your stuck money is likely to be revived this week. You need to spend a part of your money on

yourself as you have the right of being a self-made person. You need to enjoy the luxuries that you get out of your hard work. You will be satisfied with the way you have been implementing your plans on time. You will see the results in some time soon. 'Three of Cups' says that this is the time to celebrate a recent victory and go ahead by enjoying the time with your loved ones. You will get a much-needed break from your work too. 'The High Priestess' is asking you to be more active by using your capabilities and your potential in a right manner so that you do not waste your energy by being idle.

Love
You are likely to get highly negative about someone which might lead to some misunderstandings. You need to be clear from your side before you come to conclusions.

Money
'Ace of Cups' says that you will be enjoying all the monetary and the material gains this week to the maximum. You might even spend a lot on your near and dear ones which will lead to mental satisfaction.

Health
Health needs your time and patience. You need to be regular with your medication so that there is no fault from your side.

Career

You have to take out ample time so that you get to know about the pros and cons of the situations by analyzing them to the fullest.

Education

Those who are waiting for some results might have to be a little more patient as they will get to hear good news.

Lucky numbers

1 and 3

Lucky colour

Earthly Brown

Lucky days

Monday, Tuesday and Friday

Remedies

Health needs attention this week. You need to convert negativity into positivism and this can be done by meditating and being more into spiritualism. You have to be very patient this week so that there are no misunderstandings cropping up in relations too. Accept the work that comes in your way with dedication. You need to spend some more time with your loved ones.

27th Week
(June 28 to July 4)

Overview

'The Empress' says that this week, you will be going out and helping others fulfill their wishes with ease and pleasure. You will not hesitate to lend a helping hand and satisfy others. At the start of the week, diplomacy and manipulations will help you go through a difficult situation. You need to handle the situation with wit and cleverness. You will be emotional and also focused and in this way your work will not get affected this week. You will be enjoying and celebrating time with your family and friends. Your family will be enjoying your presence and company. 'Ten of Wands' says that you shall not over-burden yourself as it will lead to unwanted mental tension and health problems. You need to share these responsibilities with others and concentrate on much important work. You will be full of positive power and exuberance and this attitude of yours is likely to impress your seniors. You will be moving ahead and taking the next steps with positive and a good mind-frame. You shall not help others if they are ready to respect and value your words. You need to help only those who have faith in your efforts and abilities.

Love
You will be battling out some confusions this week. Make sure that you are clearly talking and expressing your feelings and thoughts.

Money
Money matters will be managed with care and prosperity. You will be enjoying the rewards this week.

Health
Health will be fine this week. You will be working throughout and this will keep you active.

Career
Career graph will be going upward as per your wish. You will enjoy the environment as it satisfies your needs and wants.

Education
You will have to be a lot more innovative so that your ideas can come out. You need to express your willingness by showing more interest and taking up the new things with more confidence.

Lucky numbers
9 and 8

Lucky colour
Magenta Pink

Lucky days
Monday, Tuesday and Thursday

Remedies
You may be facing some tensions in love-life which might even lead to a communication gap and as a result, you may be unable to concentrate on other important things too. You can gift others or a close person, a sim card and avoid any sort of miscommunication or communication gap. You can even place a Quartz Pyramid this week at the table as it will enhance your relations in a positive way. You also need to develop a sense of appreciation for others.

28th Week
(July 5 to 11)

Overview
This week, you need to be among people so that you are able to share your ideas with others and go ahead with your aim in mind. You need to be with people whom you love and care for. You have to be a lot more interactive and expressive. You need to take full care before signing any deal with a new person this week as you may be deceived. You have to be careful while taking investment decisions. 'The Moon' says that you have to keep aside your ego and doubt so that you are able to move ahead with a positive frame of mind and

on the right path. You need to be confident and do not get jealous on the success of other people. You will be taking out time to teach and guide others with your experience and knowledge. You will be respected for your words. You need to be among people and your loved ones. You might be moving away from your emotional bondages this week due to work which is a negative sign. 'The Hanged Man' says that you have to be determined this week so that confusion does not strike at you. You will be spiritual this week. You will have a good time while evaluating and enjoying the results that come your way. You might be indecisive this week but you can solve out the matter by discussing these matters with your near ones so that they will be able to guide you in the right direction.

Love
You will be extremely romantic and emotional at heart. You will be taking out a lot of time for your partner/spouse and seek emotional satisfaction.

Money
'Page of Cups' says that you will be very enjoyable and jovial this week with your finances in hand. You need to deal with a lot more maturity in the money matters.

Health
You may create problems and tensions for yourself this

week unnecessarily. Your positive attitude will change your health to the positive.

Career
Your analysis will not prove you wrong this week. You will be careful while taking major career decisions.

Education
'The Emperor' says that you shall not go ahead and help others unnecessarily as you will fall behind in that case.

Lucky numbers
5 and 3

Lucky colour
Sky Blue

Lucky days
Tuesday and Friday

Remedies
You may be thinking that you are the best and as a result your ego is likely to come in between you and others this week. You may be concentrating too much on love matters. You need to be on the right track so that you get through your dreams on time. You need to take help from your partner this week and do not go into that path where you do not have much knowledge. You need to upgrade your knowledge so that you do not lose on some important points.

29th Week
(July 12 to 18)

Overview

'Two of Cups' indicates that this week, you will be intimate towards your partner and you are likely to get closer for a deeper commitment. You need to invest your money in the right direction without much delay as it will give you high returns and good benefits. You need to put your money and resources to the right use. You are likely to enjoy and even gain higher at the monetary and at the material level this week. You have to make full and sufficient use of your money. You will be thinking about your past and in this way you are likely to lose out on some valuable opportunities this week. You have to be aware of your surroundings and respond accordingly. You might get negative this week. You need to trust your instincts and intuition powers this week so that you move ahead smoothly. You shall not trust others and get unduly influence by others. You will see a major change in your surrounding this week which is likely to surprise you. You need to be aware of the changes that take place in your environment and then take remedial actions on time. You will be ready to move ahead but a delay might not allow you to take that step. You have to be more willing and dedicated towards your aim. You will be able to cope up this weekend and enjoy your time among your friends and family. You will be the person who will bring smiles on others faces.

Love
You will be enjoying your love-life but not to the fullest. You need to make use of the resources that you get this week.

Money
You are likely to face minor troubles on your way to the financial upgradation but you will be able to sort out these problems with ease.

Health
You have to take care of your health this week and this can be done by detaching yourself from the past and move along with your present time. You will be relieved of mental tension.

Career
You might go on the opposite track as you may not have full knowledge about what you do this week. You have to be highly careful before taking on extra responsibilities.

Education
You will be going in for a deeper upgradation this week as you will concentrate with full dedication and focus.

Lucky numbers
1, 4 and 7

Lucky colour
Lotus Pink

Lucky days
Monday and Saturday

Remedies
You need to hold the financial matters in the right way. You have to be among people whom you love so that you do not get depressed. There may be a lot of confusion in your love life too. You have to enhance your career prospects by using more of blues this week at the career place and at home. You can even place a movable object at the work place for you as you have to adjust yourself to the societal changes this week.

30th Week
(July 19 to 25)

Overview
A lot of hard work and action is coming up this week which will keep you busy and your life may seem hectic. You will make the most of this week and you will get positive results in the future. You need to be away from people who are of negative frame of mind and outlook.

You have to be a lot more interactive and not discreet as you will gain more if you are able to interact with people at the right time by exchanging your views. Make sure you have full information needed and then you take on the steps with confidence. Avoid committing minor mistakes as it might have a huge impact on you. You will go on helping others at home and at the office which will improve your public image and also will earn respect and regard from others. You will enjoy this time with others. You will get justice to the hard work done till now and you will be satisfied with the results that you get this week. 'The World' says that you have the blessings of all the supreme powers and this is a very prosperous week for you to start on with new and exciting work. You will do good work this week and help the needy too. You will share the gains that you enjoy with others.

Love
Love-life will be extremely happening this week. You will be enjoying each and every moment that comes your way.

Money
'Queen of Pentacles' says that you will take out some time and money for yourself from your earning and enjoy the benefits. Spend within limits.

Health
Your health will be good this week without giving any trouble. Those who are not well will see positive changes in their health.

Career
Career matters need a lot of care this week. You need not sacrifice unnecessarily for others as your aim will suffer that way.

Education
You have to be practical and take on one subject at one time so as to avoid confusions and chaos. You shall aim at long-term benefits.

Lucky numbers
2, 6 and 7

Lucky colour
Sea Green

Lucky days
Thursday, Friday and Saturday

Remedies
There may be a downfall at the career front or things may not be moving according to your expectations this week. You have to check whether your efforts are being utilized in the right manner or not.

31st Week
(July 26 to August 1)

Overview

'Ten of Wands' says that you might be over pressurizing yourself by taking on some extra responsibilities unwantedly. You need to share and divide your tasks among your colleagues so as to get the accurate result. You can go ahead and implement the plans and move ahead as you are likely to come up on the top with your bright ideas by impressing others. A person close to you will be of immense help to you this week. You need to have a positive frame of mind. 'Seven of Wands' says that this week, you will be working a lot harder towards the attainment of your goals and this will keep you busy. You will have to be more interactive and enjoy the time which you spend with others. You shall project and advertise your ideas and views with others and also welcome suggestions from others. 'Six of Pentacles' says that you will be enjoying the luxuries and the pleasures that you get this week through monetary and material benefits. You have to change your attitude and be more flexible this week. At the end of the week, you will see a big change in the environment around. You have to be positive during this week and take on the changes with a positive frame of mind.

Love
You will be emotional and sentimental. You will be highly bubbly and will enjoy the time with your family and friends.

Money
You shall not be self-centered as you might have to spend a part of your money on others.

Health
Health will suffer if you do not take extra care of yourself. You need to spend wherever necessary.

Career
Career graph will see a downfall if there is even a slight negligence on your part.

Education
'The Moon' says that you shall not think about the progress of others as it will hinder your progress at the education centre.

Lucky numbers
1 and 8

Lucky colour
Grey

Lucky days
Sunday, Monday and Thursday

Remedies

You need to take care of the steps that you take at the career front this week. You may be feeling as if 'Once bitten twice shy'. You have to take risk and move ahead. Have confidence on your abilities and move forward with a positive mental frame. You may not be getting the desired results but for better results you have to find out a way which can be done by keeping a Blue evil eye with you at house or a Silver wind chime at the North West direction at home.

32nd Week
(August 2 to 8)

Overview

'Queen of Pentacles' says that you might go on to spend some percentage of your money on yourself to pamper yourself, but you also need to keep in mind that you have to follow a proper budget so as to avoid any kind of unwanted expenditures. You will be enjoying the time when you come across some new and more gains this week. 'The Chariot' says that you can surely plan an outing with your friends or family members this week. You are likely to go ahead with a positive note and achieve your goals on time. You need to be careful and do not compromise for others as this would yield you anything but a downfall. You should know how to diplomatically say No and manage some situations. You need to make investment plans this week as sitting idle will not be beneficial. You have been evaluating your gains for sometime and now is the time for some action. 'The Magician' says that you will be the heart of most of the social events as you will manage to make a light moment wherever you go. People around you will enjoy your company. You need to slow down the pace as you are full of extra energy. You need to keep some energy for reserve and move slowly and steadily so that you are able to make a note of the changes that take place in the surroundings. You will be passionate and intimate towards a special person towards the end of the week. You will enjoy the week with your family and close ones.

Love
You will be enthusiastic and energetic towards your relations and you will be satisfied with the way your love life is proceeding.

Money
'The Empress' says that you will help others with what you have in hand. Your sharing nature will be a plus point this week.

Health
You might be having some mental tensions this week which might take your time and as a result your health is likely to suffer.

Career
'Five of Wands' says that you will face a competition this week at the office front. There is likely to be a lot of work that is coming your way.

Education
You are likely to get offers this week for upgradation which have to be considered seriously so that you get to improve your knowledge from time to time.

Lucky numbers
1 and 9

Lucky colour
Golden Yellow

Lucky days
Sunday, Monday and Thursday

Remedies
There are competitions this week. You are likely to face health problems too. You can wear a Black Turbuline pendent this week so as to keep away from negativity. You can even keep a bowl full of salt in your bath room as it will absorb all the negativity from your

environment. You have to write down a positive affirmation on a Yellow piece of paper with a Red pen and make an aeroplane out of it. The height to which the aeroplane flies will be the time within which your wish will come true. You need to think positive this week.

33rd Week
(August 9 to 15)

Overview
'Five of Swords' says that you need to take on one task at a time so that you do not go for shortcuts and short termed benefits. You need to analyze each and every situation fully and then take the steps one by one. You need to be in the vigilance and company of people who are positive and have an encouraging attitude. You will be benefited, if you are in a positive environment. You need to work with full concentration and dedication so that you get the accurate results instead of halfhearted results. You need to be more practical while applying knowledge. You need to have full and deep knowledge before you take up any new objective this week otherwise you shall go in the opposite direction which might even be aimless. 'Six of Cups' says that you will be encouraging people around you by providing them

with what they need and want. You will satisfy the wants of the people around. You will get justice to the energy you have put in different directions. As the week proceeds you will see many positive things taking place around you. 'Seven of Swords' says that the weekend might end on different note if you do not take care of the tasks that are being assigned to you. You need to make an aim and work towards it with dedication. Do not mix up all the things together.

Love
You need to be aware of the fact that you have everything round and you need to utilize all that in your favour and enjoy the week with your family and friends.

Money
'The Temperance' says that you will handle the money matters with pleasure and ease.

Health
You will be emotional and that will be reflecting on your health too. You will enjoy the week to the fullest with your health giving you no trouble.

Career
'Queen of Swords' says that you will have to be a lot more analytical and careful while taking decisions. You have to analyze the situations from all prospects.

Education
'Four of Wands' says that you are likely to come to a completion this week and you will be highly pleased and satisfied with the results.

Lucky numbers
5 and 7

Lucky colour
Lilac

Lucky days
Wednesday, Thursday and Friday

Remedies
You need to go on for an upgradation this week. There has to be an enhancement regarding spiritualism. You will notice that whatever you say, things will take place accordingly. You are blessed and hence you need to do good things. You have to balance your Karmas and this can be done if you do good deeds. You have to share your ideas and opinions with others. You can go to an orphanage and distribute chocolates among children.

34th Week
(August 16 to 22)

Overview
'Ace of Wands' says that this week will be amazingly

positive for students. Those who are planning for further higher studies will get positive response if waiting. You might come across some initial problems but you will sail through with a positive attitude and by using your experiences in a right manner. You will be able to sort out all the difficulties. You will take out time to implement your plans and your ideas on the right track. You will succeed in all the undertakings that you take. You need to get detached from your past in order to move ahead with ease. You have to live in the present and work for the future. You have to forget your past in order to move ahead. You might come across some delays, but the reason lies within. You need to develop a more positive outlook and show more dedication and willingness to work harder. You need to surrender yourself so that you are able to work with full focus and concentration. You need to invest this week so that you do not face any long stagnation.

Love

You will be enjoying a good and a strong position in your love-affairs and you will be influential to some of your close ones.

Money

'Two of Cups' says that you will enjoy the gains that you get this week. You are even likely to spend some percent of your income on your close persons.

Health
'Four of Cups' says that living in the past will disturb you and your health. You need to move on and take on the challenges that come your way. As a result you will enjoy the time and you will have a good health.

Career
You need to stay positive with regard to your career prospects so that you do not lose on important chances to prove your abilities in front of others. Do not listen to others as they might have a negative effect on you.

Education
'Ace of Pentacles' says that you will be enjoying the rewards this week for the work that you do at the educational institute. You will go on for further studies if any plans are to be implemented.

Lucky numbers
4 and 6

Lucky colour
Maroon

Lucky days
Monday, Tuesday and Thursday

Remedies
You need to care and nurture the work that you do this week. Commitments need to be fulfilled on time. You

can go ahead and provide medicines at the hospital or the needy and fulfill their medication needs.

35th Week
(August 23 to 29)

Overview
'Knight of Swords' says that you will be full of energy and positive vibe and you will continuously move ahead with focus. You will be enthusiastic and excited to go ahead with a vibe in you. You will be analyzing each and every step that you take this week. You shall not get any difficulties in your path as you will not leave any scope for mistakes. You will be enjoying the fruits and the gains that you get this week but make sure that you make others a part of your happiness and share your fruits and benefits with them too. 'The Sun' says that you will be on high as all aspects of life will be going according to expectations. You need to make investment decisions this week so that you do not repent after losing bright opportunities. 'Nine of Cups' says that you will be analyzing and enjoying the fruits of your hard work and as a result you will be satisfied with the results too. 'Three of Swords' says that you need to be highly positive towards the end of the week

so that you do not create hurdles for yourself. You need to be focused too.

Love
'Ten of Cups' indicates that you will be family-oriented this week. You will not leave any scope for complaints from your family side.

Money
'The Emperor' says that you need to look after your priorities and first satisfy your own needs and then go on helping others.

Health
You need to take care of yourself and go on taking regular check-ups as health is likely to give you problems.

Career
You will be like a teacher and a helping hand to some of your juniors and you will be respected for your words.

Education
You might be over-pressurizing yourself unnecessarily this week. You have to take on one task at a time for perfection.

Lucky numbers
1 and 7

Lucky colour
Green

Lucky days
Wednesday, Thursday and Friday

Remedies
Do not keep yourself over-occupied as it will not result in accurate and the expected results. You need to take happiness from your environment and get satisfied. You can even take a holiday and take the much-needed break and take rest. During this time, you can even analyze your position and take remedial steps.

36th Week
(August 30 to September 5)

Overview
'The Star' says that one of your dearest wishes is likely to come true this week. You will be excited all through and this will result in a positive environment too. You will be emotional but you need to express your true feelings to others and then move forward. People should come to know about your feelings and innermost desires. You need to be among your loved ones and do not try to move away from them. You shall be interactive and expressive. 'The Hanged Man' indicates that you will be spiritual this week. But some double thoughts or confusions may keep you busy or tensed. You need

to have confidence on your abilities and also you need to discuss your problem with your close associates so that you get valuable suggestions. 'Knight of Cups' says that you will be focused and as a result your positive attitude will keep you away from obstacles. You will move on strongly towards your aim and destination. You will get the desired results. You shall not go out of the way in order to help others as you are likely to get sadness in return you need to be specific and help only those who respect your words. Your energy will be going through and people around you will get to learn from you. You have to be a little more mature so that you do not commit any unwanted small mistakes.

Love
'Three of Wands' says that you will be having a happy-go-lucky time with your family and friends. You will be in touch with your close ones and as a result you will be positive

Money
You will be celebrating this week and as a result your financial position will not let you down.

Health
Your health will be fine but you can surely enhance it by being more active and fast. You might be idle which is likely to keep you low.

Career

You may get highly negative about a particular case at the career front which will affect you in a negative manner. You need to keep your spirits high so as to be positive.

Education

'The Judgment' says that students who are waiting for results will get to hear the result they deserve and as a result you can even plan for future.

Lucky numbers

3 and 8

Lucky colour

Turquoise

Lucky days

Sunday and Wednesday

Remedies

You might see your career options getting blocked. You need to take a pause from your daily routine this week. You have to do the work where your interest lies. You need to use your capabilities in a right manner without letting it go to waste. Take proper advice from your elders and take guidance.

37th Week
(September 6 to 12)

Overview

'The World' says that you will have all the things which you need this week and yet you will have no shortage of love and opportunities too. You need to use these opportunities and blessings in a positive manner. You will see a big reversal in the situations around you and as a result you are likely to come across some new beginnings too. You might be moving a bit fast too especially after so many changes. You need to analyze the situations and then move forward. You will be spiritual this week and in this way you need to use your powers to come out of a double-thought situation so that confusion does not take much of your vital time. 'Eight of Pentacles' says that you have to take out time some money out of you income and spend some on your self-enhancement so that you get a chance to satisfy your own personal needs too. You will go on ahead with a positive force and as a result you will be happily succeeding. 'The Tower' indicates that you shall not sacrifice so much that in the end you only fall from your current position leading to dishearten. You need to look after your own priorities and goals. You have to take care of your health so that you do not get ill while looking after other people.

Love
'The Fool' says that you will be enthusiastic and eager to move forward with your relations. You will enjoy this phase.

Money
'Queen of Pentacles' says that you are likely to spend some part of your income on yourself but you have to follow a budget so as to avoid any frivolous expenditure.

Health
'Six of Cups' says that you will be taking care and supporting others through out the week. People around you will respect your efforts.

Career
You need to collect all the deep information and knowledge before you take up any decision as you are tended to take the wrong route.

Education
You will see a completion taking place this week. You will be glad with the outcome and you will enjoy the fruits too.

Lucky numbers
4 and 3

Lucky colour
Black

Lucky days
Monday, Thursday and Saturday

Remedies
There may be some problems in your career line. Do not take up any work without having even the slightest knowledge about it. You need to take out the negative thoughts out of your mind. You have to be confident and trust your abilities. Take suggestions and respect what others' say. Take out each step slowly. You can keep a Blue evil eye with you so as to avoid any negative feelings.

38th Week
(September 13 to 19)

Overview
'The Wheel of Fortune' says that you have to set your mind on one aim and go ahead with fully concentrating and focusing without thinking much about the results and putting in your full efforts. You will be highly romantic this week and as a result you are likely to go ahead for a deeper commitment. You can even initiate new relations. 'The Judgment' says that you need to wait for the results and leave everything to God as you have done your part of the work. You need to express yourself and go ahead sharing your true feelings with

everyone. You have to be interactive. You need to be manipulative and diplomatic so that your work goes ahead without any problem. You will be helping and guiding others so that they are able to tackle the problems that they face with ease. You will show light to others and you will be respected and reciprocated positively. You need to be more dedicated and willing towards what you take up this week so that you move ahead without any delay. A third person close to you will be of immense help and you need to take it in a positive way.

Love
'The Sun' says that you will be full of vibe and strength and in this way you will get a positive response in return.

Money
'Queen of Cups' says that you need to be positive this week and do not trust others as far as your investment decisions are concerned.

Health
You will be highly energetic and enthusiastic this week and this attitude will reflect on your health too.

Career
You might create some unwanted obstacles for yourself if you doubt on your capabilities and potential. You need to have full confidence on your abilities so that you do not lose on some vital offers.

Education
You will be helping others and guiding them with their work. You will be glad to help others as your efforts will be recognized.

Lucky numbers
1 and 3

Lucky colour
Lilac

Lucky days
Monday, Tuesday and Wednesday

Remedies
Do not have any doubt regarding your career. You should not act or react. You have to change your perspective towards other things in life so as to move forward. You can donate Purple cloth at the temple or even feed a needy by giving them grapes.

39th Week
(September 20 to 26)

Overview
'Knight of Cups' says that you will be emotional plus focused too. You will take active participation in the events that take place around you this week. You will be looking for a higher target this week after enough

evaluation. You will be happy with the way you have performed till now and now you will focus on higher degree. Do not take up many responsibilities at a time as it will have a negative effect on your health. You need to share and delegate your tasks on others too and give others their share of work. You will be family-oriented this week and you are likely to take out a lot of time for your family. You will be highly romantic and sentimental too. You will see an inclination towards a specific person this week. 'Ace of Pentacles' says that you might come across material and monetary benefits this week and you will be enjoying the fruits of your labour. This is the perfect time to make investment enhancements. You can even invest in property. You might have to move away from your emotional bondages this week which might keep you dull. You need to understand that you have to make sacrifices so as to gain in the future. You will be an impressive person at the work place and at the social circle. You will be spreading smiles and creating a light environment wherever you go.

Love
You might try too many things at a time which is likely to create a total chaos and confusion. Take one person at a time and talk patiently without getting impulsive this week.

Money

You have to be highly careful while managing your gains this week so that you do not commit any small mistake this week. These small mistakes are likely to take a big form in the future if you are negligent.

Health

You have to be among positive people so that negativity does not influence you. Negativity around you is likely to affect your health badly.

Career

You might be seeing initial obstacles which will be cleared without much effort too. You have to be determined and strong.

Education

You need to keep aside your ego and move ahead without thinking much about the progress of others. You shall concentrate on your aims and move ahead with faith and hope.

Lucky numbers

1 and 8

Lucky colour

Deep Red

Lucky days

Tuesday, Wednesday and Saturday

Remedies

There is a complete change needed in your love life, monetary position and health condition. You may be too much questioning and this might create hurdles for you. Do not doubt on small things and cut down from your ego so as to move ahead. You need to be among your relations. You can use Red colour this week to enhance your energy level and you can even gift flowers to a close person and make them happy.

40th Week
(September 27 to October 3)

Overview

'King of Swords' says that your analytical power will be highly important and effective this week. You will be analyzing each and every aspect very carefully and this will help you gain a good and a strong position. You need to share your benefits and the gains that you enjoy with others and make their presence felt around you. 'Five of Cups' says that you need to detach yourself from your past and move on by holding your present in the right form with a positive attitude. You shall not go on helping people while earning a bad name. You need to see whether people around you respect your words or not. You have to concentrate on your priorities. You will be successfully implementing your ideas at the right time without fail. 'Knight of Pentacles' says that do not get attached to your earnings. You need to invest at the right time without fail. You will be highly satisfied with the outcomes of the work you do this week. You will be slowly evaluating your performance at ease. 'Five of Wands' says that you will be facing stiff competition this week which will keep you busy. You need to take out time so that you can plan your steps from time to time and go further without feeling the pressure.

Love
You need to take action this week and be responsive so that you get the right reaction.

Money
'The Temperance' says that you will be able to balance and maintain your financial position very well.

Health
You need to take out time for your heath this week. Negativity is likely to influence you this week. You shall be open to people and their suggestions too.

Career
You shall be analyzing and evaluating but you need to use all your inputs and intellect in the right manner without fail.

Education
'The High Priestess' says that you have plenty of ideas

but these ideas will be helpful and fruitful only when you work on them. Be active and take action.

Lucky numbers
2, 5 and 9

Lucky colour
Golden Yellow

Lucky days
Sunday, Tuesday and Friday

Remedies
You are having fixed ideas about some people or work. You need not be self-centered instead you have to be giving and helping others more whenever possible. You shall note the entire positive and the negative aspects before coming to conclusions. You shall not depend on others for your work. You need to confess your love and express your true feelings so as to get the clear picture from others too. You can meet your mentor this week and seek blessings from them.

41st Week
(October 4 to 10)

Overview
'Nine of Wands' says that you will be happily and successfully implementing your plans in a right manner.

You need to come out of a double thought situation this week by telling out and sharing your ideas with your close people so that you feel lighter and at peace. 'The Devil' says that you shall not get highly motivated towards a person as it will add to your negative attitude and you need to realize that you have many offers in hand which need to be considered with positive attitude. Do not keep thinking about the past as it will affect you mentally. 'Four of Wands' says that you will notice that all your incomplete projects will get completed this week with an ease. 'The Chariot' is indicating a trip this week either due to work or relations. You will be spiritual this week. You need to take care while getting into new deals as it will affect your performance if there is any kind of negligence on your part. You will be enjoying a decent and a strong position at the end of the week. You will be respected and adored for the way you work.

Love
You will be highly happy and satisfied with your love life this week. You will get all the support that you need.

Money
'Two of Swords' says that you need to welcome suggestions and advice from your close associates and then take the final decisions regarding money matters.

Health
Health will be on a high this week. You will be enjoying the time and seek pleasure.

Career
'Seven of Wands' says that you are ready to work hard this week and you will definitely see positive response from our seniors.

Education
'The Star' says that you will see a dream come true and as a result you will enjoy the fruits that come by you this week. Education advancement will be on the right path.

Lucky numbers
4 and 7

Lucky colour
Peacock Blue

Lucky days
Thursday and Saturday

Remedies
There is a need for exchange of money this week. You need to market your abilities and work up till now so as to seek more response and work for you. You need to mingle with more people and say positive things as they will affect you. Do not be lonely this week as it will

not be good for you mentally. You can keep Chinese coins tied with a Red thread or a red ribbon and keep it in your wealth corner.

42nd Week
(October 11 to 17)

Overview

You will be on a high this week especially your emotions on your mind. You will be enthusiastic this week regarding the building of new relations. You are encouraged to work harder and take up new jobs this week as you will definitely excel in the new undertakings this week. You have to be careful before taking the new route, as you need to make sure any new plans before implemented, you have to check it with your elders and seniors as they will guide you properly. 'Queen of Pentacles' says that you might go ahead and spend some part of your income on yourself and then pamper yourself. You will get an opportunity to satisfy your needs this week. 'Eight of Swords' says that you need to mix up with people and advertise how you perceive things. You should let others know about your point of views. You are likely to get the right kind of offers which would match your qualification and interests too. You have to take up these offers and prove your abilities. 'The Justice' card implies that you will get justice if you are caught up with a legal matter this week. You will be enjoying the monetary benefits that come your way. Make sure you make some useful plans by using these gains in the right manner.

Love
A highly cherishable time this week will be. You will see some beautiful moments with your life-partner

Money
'Three of Cups' says that the money matters will be handled in a positive manner. You will even plan a celebration this week.

Health
You will enjoy good health this week but some more activity will surely enhance your health to the positive.

Career
'The Lovers' says that you will take up the job at the office with pleasure and deep interest.

Education
You will be having a ball at the education centre as everything will go according to your expectations. You will be encouraged to work harder.

Lucky numbers
1 and 6

Lucky colour
Yellow

Lucky days
Sunday, Friday and Saturday

Remedies
There is a need for charity this week. You can donate Yellow cloth or food this week to the needy and satisfy their needs. You can even donate Yellow sweets or laddoo or even banana or mango.

43rd Week
(October 18 to 24)

Overview
This week will be highly spiritual for you. You will seek mental satisfaction his week. You will be encouraged to move forward and you will also work with dedication. You need to get detached from your bitter past so as to move ahead. You might go on helping people for very little gains and for name and fame. 'The Moon' says that you need to keep aside your ego and doubt so as to move ahead with ease. Do not get affected by the progress and concentrate on your aim. You will be looked forward and people will enjoy your company this week. You will also take active participation in the events that take place around. 'Three of Cups' says that this week

is a time to celebrate and enjoy. You will take pride in your work and you will be recognized for your efforts. You will now take out time to study how you have been faring these many weeks and you will come to a final conclusion. You will be happy with the results that you come to know. 'Ace of Pentacles' says that at the end of the week, you might come across some monetary gains and this will keep you elated and happy.

Love
Your love-life will be going ahead smoothly and you will have no complaints with your relations. New relations will be high and blooming.

Money
You need to mix up and be interactive so that you come to know about the positive and the negative points of your work.

Health
'Page of Wands' says that your health will be highly positive and your enthusiasm will come out this week.

Career
Career matters will be a matter of high concern this week. You need to look before you leap and take remedial measures.

Education
You may have to opt the other way so that you are able to accomplish your targets on time this week.

Lucky numbers
1 and 9

Lucky colour
Sea Green

Lucky days
Wednesday, Thursday and Saturday

Remedies
You need to hold your money in a right manner so that you do not lose on it. Apply and make use of your money in the right direction. You need to manage your money flow in the right way. This week, you may have to butter some of your fellowmen. You can wear a sphatic necklace this week or even enhance your environment with Green colour for overall prosperity.

44th Week
(October 25 to 31)

Overview
'Six of Pentacles' says that you will be helping out people with what you have in hand. You will be happy as people around you will go on and ask your support. You need to realize that you have everything in hand and you need to utilize every element in the positive manner. You need to take investment decisions on time

so that you are able to manage your future with security and surety. You need to make immediate plans for investments. 'King of Pentacles' says that you have to become detached to your gains in order to help the needy and the poor. You have to make some arrangements so that you can lend a helping hand to the needy. You will go on and be a pillar of support to many people this week. You will not hesitate to help and support others. 'The Hierophant' indicates that you might even teach your juniors by using your experience and intellect. People around you will be very thankful and will respect your efforts. You will be extremely happy this week as one of your prolonged wishes is likely to come true and as a result you will be active and adorable. You will be working during the weekend too. You will work harder and this will give you a sense of satisfaction and achievement.

Love
You might have to go away from your emotions. You need to be in touch with your close ones so that there is no communication gap.

Money
You will handle the inflow of money very well. You will be continuously making future plans but do not think for a long time.

Health

Health will keep you tensed. You need to take care and have proper rest as you are likely to get stressed out.

Career

'The Lovers' says that you will be highly involved in the tasks assigned to you this week. You are likely to leave no scope for improvement.

Education

You are likely to get highly negative this week with your education on mind. You will be losing out on some vital opportunities if you do not change your attitude.

Lucky numbers

4 and 8

Lucky colour

Earthly Brown

Lucky days

Sunday, Wednesday and Friday

Remedies

You might be leaving your emotions behind. You need to realize that you will be happier if you have a person supporting you as there is a saying that after every successful man, there is a woman. You need to take this into account. You have to go out and meet people so that you get to project your ideas in the true form.

45th Week
(November 1 to 7)

Overview
You have to stop sacrificing this week. You might even lose what you have in hand by helping and compromising for others. This will be highly prosperous week for those who want to start with a new job, project or a new course as their stars will help them come on the top successfully. 'The Emperor' says that you might even help people by neglecting yourself. This in return is likely to affect your health in a negative way. You will be spiritual but you need to use this positive power so that you do not face any dilemma this week. 'King of Cups' says that you have to be a lot more expressive and interactive. Let go your true feelings in the air so that people know your actual and true personality. You need not trust people and let them influence you as you are likely to get affected by negativity. You need to be careful and trust only your instincts and intuition. If waiting for results, you will be blessed with positive results. You have to work with more willingness and dedication so as to avoid any kind of delays.

Love
You have to spend some percentage of your income on your loved ones too this week and help them satisfy their personal needs.

Money

You will enjoy a good and strong position as far as your monetary level is concerned. You will be happy as you will be enjoying the fruits of the work done.

Health

Your health will be highly positive this week. You will seek mental satisfaction and this will reflect on your health too.

Career

You will be enjoying this week by taking pride and deep interest in your work.

Education

'Knight of Swords' says that you might have to slow down so that you get to learn new things and enhance your knowledge with ease.

Lucky numbers

4 and 8

Lucky colour

Earthly Brown

Lucky days

Sunday, Wednesday and Friday

Remedies

You have to accept the work and be more responsible and committed towards the work assigned. You shall not be straight forward as people around you may get hurt by your words. You need to give others a chance to advertise their suggestions too. You can listen to soft and smooth music everyday in the morning as it will revitalize you and keep your mind fresh the whole day.

46th Week
(November 8 to 14)

Overview
'Seven of Swords' says that you have to be careful while choosing your line of work as you tend to choose the wrong line. You will be enthusiastic and energetic this week while taking up new work especially related to finances. You need to be among people so that you get an audience to advertise your thoughts. You might be in a deep mess this week as a close person is likely to get on you and even break your trust. You have to choose the person who is true and then disclose important information. You need to avoid being in the company of people who have a negative influence on you. 'Five of Swords' says that you shall be in a hurry to finish all the tasks but you need to understand that this will lead to chaos and not perfection. You need to take on one thing at a time so that you finish one thing at a time. 'Three of Wands' says that you will be taking out time so that you get to think about the further needed steps.

You have to be careful and aware of your past performance too. You might create some obstacles for yourself if you do not change your attitude from negative to positive. You need to rely on the people around and work by having full confidence on on the work that you do.

Love
You will be enjoying the week with your close ones paying attention to your needs and wants.

Money
'The Death card' says that this week, money matters will make a trouble for you if you do not pay deep and complete attention to your finances.

Health
Health will be highly positive and energetic. You can take up new tasks this week as your health will favour you.

Career
'Ace of Swords' says that you will be on the top this week with your career being a highlight of the week.

Education
Education will be a top priority for you this week. Students are going to perform extremely well this week.

Lucky numbers
3 and 8

Lucky colour
Ocean Blue

Lucky days
Sunday and Friday

Remedies
There may be hurdles this week in the money department. Those who are planning to change their job can go further and opt for a new line too. You need to be more disciplined and organized with your work lined up properly. You can donate books to the needy and enlighten their mind with knowledge and as a result you will be blessed. You will get positive results.

47th Week
(November 15 to 21)

Overview
'Six of Cups' says that you will be helping out people with their problems and you will not hesitate to fulfill and satisfy the needs of your close ones. You will see positive results coming your way this week. Those who are fighting legal cases can expect a positive turn. You have to open your eyes and realize that you are being offered with good and bright opportunities and this can be done if you are able to stop thinking about your

past and start thinking about your present and future. You need to surrender yourself to the work that you take up so that you are able to establish your plans and ideas with confidence and faith. You will be back on the track and now after deep evaluation you will go on to implement your plans successfully. You need to put in the desired amount of efforts and invest on time so that you do not get stagnated in the middle of the road. You are likely to face an examination or an appraisal test this week which will be like a competition. You have to take up this challenge and work accordingly. By the end of the week, you will see everything back on the track. You will be highly satisfied with the results and now you will enjoy the weekend with pleasure.

Love

You will be analyzing your love relations. You need to give time and space and do not analyze or evaluate your relations as these are not mind game.

Money

Money level will be highly supportive this week. You will enjoy the week with the financial sector supporting you fully.

Health

'Page of Cups' says that you will be elated and excited this week and this attitude will surely reflect in your health and overall personality. You will enjoy good health.

Career
You need to work with whole-heartedness and not on probability basis for accurate results

Education
'Ace of Cups' says that you will be deeply involved in the studies that you take up this week. Students will be extremely responsive and will take part in extra curricular activities too.

Lucky numbers
2 and 4

Lucky colour
Magenta Pink

Lucky days
Saturday and Sunday

Remedies
There is a balance needed at the heart and mind level. You have to be patient this week. You need to be cool and calm. Do not get hyper as you see changes. You can enhance your environment with White colour as it will give you peace of mind.

48th Week
(November 22 to 28)

Overview

This week, you are likely to face some minor problems but with your wit, talent and experience you will be able to clear out all these problems with ease. 'Ten of Wands' says that you might try to take up all the responsibilities on your own shoulder without giving much importance to your health. You need to take care of your health and share your tasks with others. A third person close to you might be helping you so as to finish the work on time. You are likely to get the stuck money this week which will keep you excited. You need to enter and take up a line about which you have full knowledge and information. You might even end up taking the opposite route if you do not take the proper guidance from your seniors. You will see all the incomplete and pending jobs getting completed with perfection. You can initiate new projects as your old commitments are done with. You have to open your grid and come out to see the world from a better angle. You need to be interactive and do not make your own assumptions by creating terms and conditions. 'Seven of Pentacles' says that you have to be more precise with your investments on your mind. Make sure you take decisions regarding investment plans. 'The Temperance' indicates that by the end of the week, you will see yourself spiritually inclined. You will be able to tackle all the difficulties with ease as you will know how to balance all your activities.

Love
You will take things lightly and cheerfully and this will help you enjoy your emotions and loved ones to the fullest.

Money
'Two of Cups' says that you will take deep interest in knowing the inflow and the outflow of money this week. You will handle and manage your finances nicely.

Health
'The High Priestess' says that you have to be a little more active so that you enjoy your health to the fullest.

Career
'The Sun' says that your career will shine as bright as the Sun and you will seek and enjoy all the rewards and the fruits to the fullest.

Education
You might be analyzing the situations from one side. You need to use your intellect fully and then arrive to conclusions.

Lucky numbers
2 and 4

Lucky colour
Saffron

Lucky days
Monday, Wednesday and Saturday

Remedies
You will see that everything will go according to your wishes this week. You can give a lecture on your experiences and give consultations to others by using your intellect so as to guide and help others. You need to involve others in your happiness and give others a reason to smile.

49th Week
(November 29 to December 5)

Overview
You know how and when to take vital decisions and in this way people around you will look up to you as an influential individual. You will have a strong will power and determination. You will be evaluating and analyzing your performance and you will come to know about the mistakes that can be rectified. You will be happy with the results. You need to change your attitude

to the positive as otherwise, your doubtful nature might become as a hurdle for you only. 'Nine of Pentacles' says that you are likely to come across monetary gains this week. You will enjoy and share these benefits with your close ones and take pleasure out of it. You will be romantic and seek emotional satisfaction. You may even look forward to see a special person this week. You have all the things at place; their usage has to be positive so that you do not lack commitment. You need to use the blessings of all the divine powers in such a way that you do not look back and repent. You will be ready to work hard and achieve your targets on time. You will be interested to know the deep secrets too. 'Queen of Swords' says that though you will be analytical, you may not use this power up to the mark. You need to be fully aware of the situations and analyze the situations from all the positive and the negative sides.

Love
You might see a total reversal of the things that are taking place now. You need to spend more time with your loved ones so that you do loose clarity.

Money
You will take full care of the money matters this week and will not let go any important opportunity to enhance your monetary position.

Health
Health will be fantastic this week. You will enjoy your health to the fullest.

Career
Career prospects are looking high and bright. You will be able to strike a balance between the most important and other works.

Education
'The Hermit' says that you need to look after your own educational enhancement so that you do not leave behind.

Lucky numbers
2 and 9

Lucky colour
Pink

Lucky days
Tuesday, Wednesday and Thursday

Remedies
You need to have better relations this week. You have to keep working so that you do not have any gap in between. You may be even under a difficult period as far as your love matters are concerned. You need to take out time and talk peacefully and clear out all the differences. You need to meet people and give

importance to others and their suggestions too. You can light Pink candles at home for 3-5 minutes everyday.

50th Week
(December 6 to 12)

Overview

You will be aiming higher this week. And you will not be disappointed with the results that you get this week. You will be able to come out on top with a specific project in mind. You will be the centre of attraction wherever you go this week. People around you will take lessons from you too. You are likely to face stagnation if you do not put the needed amount of money which is needed to move forward with a special project in hand. You will enjoy the week and celebrate with your family members. You will be in a jovial mood and you will be at rest too. You need to be among people who have a positive frame of mind as you are likely to get influenced by the negativity of the people around. You need to trust your inner voice and intuition this week and do not trust others. You will have to surrender yourself at the education and at the career front so as to get positive signs. You need to focus more for accurate results. 'Eight of Swords' says that you have to mingle with people and project your ideas in a right and true manner. You need to be a lot more positive and move ahead with a positive attitude. You need to express your views and feelings in front of others.

Love
You can initiate new relations this week and even think for a deeper commitment towards your partner. You will get the support of your partner/spouse.

Money
Money matters will stay positive this week and you will implement your prolonged plans accordingly.

Health
You will be enthusiastic this week and this will have a positive effect on your health.

Career
'Ten of Cups' says that you will enjoy working at the career front this week. You will take keen interest in the work that you do and as a result you are likely to get the work of your choice.

Education
You might face minor problems but these problems will not take much of your time as you will be able to clear them out on time.

Lucky numbers
3 and 6

Lucky colour
Chocolate Brown

Lucky days
Sunday, Tuesday and Saturday

Remedies
You need to be serious while taking decisions and new tasks. You have to make a serious effort so as to improve your health. You need to care and nurture the efforts that you are making. Do not take anyone for granted this week. You can write down your tasks which need to be completed each day and at the end of the day you can check your performance. You can even wear a Crystal necklace for overall balance.

51ˢᵗ Week
(December 13 to 19)

Overview
You will be moving ahead with the right spirit and the positive energy to reach your goals on time. You will be spiritual but might face some confusions or double thoughts regarding a particular issue. You need to take full care and discuss these problems with your near and dear ones so that you get vital suggestions. A third person either at the office or at home will be of immense help this week. You are likely to get back stuck money.

You will see some pending work getting completed if you take them up again. You might be in a indecisive mood. You have to take out time and closely analyze the options that you are left with. You are likely to gain monetarily this week and this gain will keep you on a high. You need to take good care of the investments that you make as you might even head towards a loss.

Love
You need to make the right move at the right time this week for the love matters.

Money
You will enjoy the time and will go on to spend some money on yourself and get pampered this week. You need to follow a proper budget so as to avoid any unwanted expenses.

Health
Health will disturb you this week if you do not take on task at a time and go on taking too much pressure at the same time. You need to give yourself proper equal rests.

Career
You have to work with full dedication and not on probability basis. You shall gain more if you work with full concentration.

Education
You will take keen interest in your studies and

upgradation. You will not leave any scope for improvement. Students have a prosperous time coming up.

Lucky numbers
3 and 5

Lucky colour
Lemon Yellow

Lucky days
Monday, Tuesday and Thursday

Remedies
You need to handle situations with maturity and practicality. You shall not try shortcuts as you will get only short-term benefits. You need to analyze the entire positive and the negative aspects before jumping to conclusions. You have to move slowly at the career front. You can wear a Metal Kada this week or else even keep a sphatic Shree-Yantra at the temple and pray in front of God.

52nd Week
(December 20 to 26)

Overview
'The Justice' says that you will get the results after waiting for long. You will get positive results from the

places where you have put in your energy and money. You will be interested to help others willingly and you will see whether others learn from your teachings in a positive way. You will come out on top and enjoy the results. A project related to intellect and mind work will take you to places. You have to come out of a grid so that you are able to analyze your position on time and then take vital steps so as to rectify the mistakes. You need to be flexible. 'Eight of Cups' says that you might have to move away from your emotional bondages due to work but this sacrifice will surely pay you in future and you will gain from all prospects. You need to gain full knowledge before you leap into any path. You will perform well if you take the full responsibility of a task and take pride while working. You need to realize that you have everything in hand and using these vital resources in a right manner will help you perform better. You need to stay positive and do not get too attached or detached with a particular work or person as it will have a depleting effect on you.

Love
You will be moving ahead smoothly. You can even plan an outing with your loved ones and enjoy some time off your work.

Money
You need to analyze your position and then move ahead

slowly. You will be benefited more if you choose to move slowly.

Health
'Seven of Swords' says that health will definitely be one of the priorities. You need to look after your health with proper medication.

Career
'Two of Pentacles' says that opportunities are likely to come your way which need to be grabbed so that you get the right platform so as to prove your capabilities.

Education
You need to make an extra effort so as to secure a strong and a secure position at the education side.

Lucky numbers
7 and 8

Lucky colour
Bright White

Lucky days
Sunday, Monday and Friday

Remedies
You may not be able to hold your emotions properly this week. You have to take the initiative and go in for upgradation. You have to make an overall balance and try to be among people this week. For improvement in

health, you need to chant the Maha Mrityunjay Mantra for 108 times everyday this week.

53rd Week
(December 27 to January 2)

Overview

You will kick start this week by being romantic and sentimental. You will get the support from your loved ones and from your near and dear ones. You need to keep your options open whenever you start new things as you will have a better idea and more opportunities. You have to change according to the changes that take place. You will be excited to help and support others and you will not hesitate to lend a helping hand to your close ones. 'Ten of Pentacles' says that you need to be more active and take important money rolling on decisions. 'King of Swords' says that you will be roaring to go ahead with a positive force. You have to be in touch with other people so that you get to know about the valuable things that happen around you. You need to stop sacrificing for others as it will not help you in any form. 'The Emperor' indicates that you even neglect yourself in order to take care of others. You first have to take care of your health and then go ahead by helping others. 'Page of Swords' says that you have to be fully equipped with all the information and knowledge before you take any further step this week otherwise you are likely to end up on the opposite side.

Love
You have to keep aside your ego this week so as to move ahead and play an important role in your relations with others.

Money
Money matters need a lot of care this week so that you do not let go any important opportunities so as to enhance your financial position.

Health
'The Magician' says that you will enjoy your health this week and go ahead by enjoying the pleasures that you get.

Career
'Ace of Pentacles' says that your career will take an upward turn and you are likely to gain materially and monetarily.

Education
You will take deep interest in learning new things this week. You will be interested to know the depths of new things that you face.

Lucky numbers
1 and 4

Lucky colour
Forest Green

Lucky days
Monday, Wednesday and Saturday

Remedies
You might have all the doors regarding money matters closed this week. You have to use your talents in a right manner so as you get the work accordingly. You have to open up and be free. Do not let your ego come in between as it will hurt you only. You can enhance this week by using more of Green colour this week in your routine. You can even plant trees and have a close contact with nature and your surroundings.

REMEDIES

1. Wealth-vase

The Wealth-vase enhances your monetary position with time. It can be made as follows-

You need to take a clear vase which would contain the picture of Goddess Laxmi on the upper side of the vase (it should be placed in such a manner that Goddess Laxmi is having a look at the bottom of the vase).

Three Chinese coins tied with a Red ribbon need to be placed inside the vase.

Fill half of the vase with semi-precious stones of seven types.

You also need to bring some quantity of mud or soil from a person whom you think is a rich person.

Place Red money or Coins in a Red packet and place it in the vase.

Next, you need to place five types of seeds or grains (wheat, rice, jowar, baajra and maize)

You also need to place ten small crystal balls in the Wealth-vase for stability.

Then papers in yellow, red, white, blue and green colour need to be cut in pieces and then kept at the bottom of the vase.

This Wealth-vase should be placed in the south-east direction of the house in such a manner that it is visible only to you and not to outsiders.

2. Vishnu Kalash

For the Vishnu Kalash the following has to be done:

Take a Copper Vessel (vase is acceptable) and place Silver coins in it on which the picture of Lord Ganesh and Goddess Laxmi are embedded.

The coins need to be placed in such a manner that the picture should be visible from the top of the mouth of the vase.

Fill the vase with water and change the water everyday.

Place Ashoka leaves and a coconut over it.

The Vishnu Kalash needs to be placed at the north-east direction of the house.

The Vishnu Kalash is also an effective way of enhancing the monetary position of the house.

3. Charity

Charity includes any kind of charity which would help you yield blessings and good wishes. You can go ahead and donate the following so as to enhance your week by doing good deeds.

- Donate books and sponsor education of a child and make a child study
- You can go ahead and even feed a needy and satisfy his/her need
- Donation involving clothes are also a very good way of making someone happy

4. Harmonic Star

'The Harmonic Star' says that you can go ahead and serve humanity. According to this, you will receive only those results aback for the work that you do. You can proceed in making the Harmonic Star by cutting the paper and making it 3 by 3. Then fold it in such a way that it becomes double and make a triangle out of it. The pin point which proceeds from the south to the north indicates that it is Humanity to God and the pin point which goes from the north to south says that it is what you receive from God. You will get what you do and thus, you should concentrate on only good deeds always. One should always say and perform good things without hurting or harming anyone.

5. Crystal

The Crystal signifies balance and stability in life. One who is facing upheavals in life can make use of any Crystal show-piece or ball and make life better and more stable. The Crystal should be placed either at the centre of the house if there is instability at the home place or at the office table if you need stability there.

Crystal involves the following objects which can affect your life in a positive way:
1. Crystal Ball
2. Crystal Shree Yantra

3. Crystal Show-piece
4. Crystal Lotus
5. Crystal Pyramid
6. Crystal Necklace
7. Crystal Pencils.

These objects will help you bring more stability and much needed balance in life and will help you look at things from a better perspective.

6. Rock salt

The use of Rock salt in our daily life will help you prevent the effect from negative vibrations that pass on from others. The Rock salt will help to absorb all the negativity from the environment around you and will help you lead a positive life. You can place a bowl full of salt in your bath room. You can sweep the floor once a week with salt water and clean the house with it so that it takes away all the negativity from your surrounding. The utilization of Rock salt is an effective way of eliminating negativity from your house.

7. Wish Pyramid

The Wish Pyramid is an effective way from which you will see your wishes coming true or close to coming true. You will have confidence and faith in your abilities and you will focus on working towards your aim in the right direction. For the Wish pyramid you need to do the following:

On a White sheet of paper you need to write down your wish with a Red pen and place it in a box which will be known as the Wish Pyramid. The wish has to be read everyday three times so that you remind yourself of your aim and continuously work towards the attainment of your aim and goals.

8. Colours

(a) Red

The Red colour is the colour of energy and vitality. The use of Red colour in our daily lives will give us the needed enthusiasm which will push us and help us to work towards our aim. You can use Red colour in your dressing style and also light Red candles everyday for 3-5 minutes as it will empower you with energy. You can even use Red fruits in your daily diet.

(b) Blue

The Blue colour brings enhancement in your career and education life. The use of Blue colour at home or at office premises will help you lead a better life at the career or at the education. You can enhance your surrounding with Blue colour by using it in your dressing style. You can also place a pair of Dolphin fishes or Madeline ducks. Placing the fountain at the office will help you give a smooth flow in your career life.

(c) Green

Green colour implies monetary enhancement and prosperity. The Green colour will give you the much needed happiness in all prospects. You can use Green colour in your daily diet by including green leafy vegetables in your diet. You can even wear Green dresses and enhance your day with vitality and prosperity.

(d) Yellow

The Yellow colour gives you clarity in your thoughts and mind process. Yellow colour will give you the courage to arrive at the right decision at the right time. You can use Yellow colour in your daily use and also in your fruit intake.

(e) Orange

Orange colour gives you strength and courage to move forward with a clear and a focused mind. You will get the power to move ahead and take the right steps. Lighting Orange colour candles will give a positive vibe in your environment and make you stronger.

(f) Purple

The Purple colour emphasizes on spirituality and divination. People who want to introduce a deeper content of spiritualism into their lives can use more of Purple colour in their lives and make a go.

(g) Pink

Pink colour indicates relations. Those who are going through a rough patch in their relations can make use of Pink and give a positive turn to their problems. You can use Pink Rose Quartz in your daily routine to enhance your life. You can even use Pink colour by wearing Pink colour dresses and also lighting Pink candles everyday for 3-5 minutes which will help you get positive energy.

Tarot... Enlightening Future

Mystical Tarot Deck
by
Dr. Seema Midha

Health & Harmony
- New Age | Tarot & Divination
- 978-81-319-0237-0
- 699pp | HB
- 5" × 6.5"
- Rs. 699.00 | US$ 63.50
- World

Distinct Features:
- Comprehensive and concise description of cards
- Fully coloured handbook
- Expressive attractive cards
- Handy and easy to understand
- Card usage has been made very simple and applicable in day to day life situations

For order & enquiries please contact :

 B. JAIN PUBLISHERS (P) LTD.
1921, Street No. 10, Chuna Mandi, Paharganj, New Delhi-110055 (India)
Tel. 91-11-2358 0800, 2358 1100, 2358 1300, 2358 3100
Fax: 91-11-2358 0471 E-mail: info@bjain.com | Web: www.bjainbooks.com

The Healing Powers of Pyramid

- Functions of Pyramid with standardized history covering realm of techniques & healing powers

Health & Harmony
- 978-81-319-0178-8
- 168 pp | PB
- Rs. 90.00

Best Sellers by
Sri Rudrabhayananda

The Hidden Mysteries of Kundalini

- Concepts of Kundalini & Chakras revealing the world of spiritual beauty & endless ecstasy

Health & Harmony
- 978-81-319-0047-5
- 460 pp | PB
- Rs. 225.00

For order & enquiries please contact :

B. JAIN PUBLISHERS (P) LTD.
1921, Street No. 10, Chuna Mandi, Paharganj, New Delhi-110055 (India)
Tel. 91-11-2358 0800, 2358 1100, 2358 1300, 2358 3100
Fax: 91-11-2358 0471 E-mail: info@bjain.com | Web: www.bjainbooks.com